THE ENGLISH CHURCH
AND THE CONTINENT

THE ENGLISH CHURCH
AND THE CONTINENT

LECTURES BY

PROFESSOR R. R. DARLINGTON
Professor of History in the University of London

THE REVD. PROFESSOR M. D. KNOWLES
*Regius Professor of Modern History
in the University of Cambridge*

W. A. PANTIN
Vice-Provost of Oriel College, Oxford

THE REVD. PROFESSOR OWEN CHADWICK
*Master of Selwyn College, Cambridge, and Dixie Professor of
Ecclesiastical History in the University of Cambridge*

THE VERY REVD.
THE DEAN OF WINCHESTER
*Formerly Dixie Professor of Ecclesiastical History
in the University of Cambridge*

THE REVD. CANON H. M. WADDAMS
*General Secretary of the Church of England
Council on Foreign Relations*

THE FAITH PRESS LTD
7 TUFTON STREET LONDON SW1

FIRST PUBLISHED IN 1959

© *The Faith Press Ltd, 1959*

PRINTED IN GREAT BRITAIN
in *11-pt. Baskerville type*
BY THE FAITH PRESS LTD
LEIGHTON BUZZARD

To the memory of
Bishop George Bell

EDITOR'S PREFACE

THE series of lectures here published on *The English Church and the Continent* was given in the Great Hall of Lambeth Palace Library in the autumn of 1957. It was inaugurated by His Grace the Archbishop of Canterbury. A glance at the table of contents will indicate the distinction of the lecturers and we appreciate our good fortune in having obtained their co-operation. Their examination of the relations between the Church in this country and the Continent will make a valuable contribution to this aspect of the history of the English Church. Another educative part of these lectures is to see how different historical minds approach similar problems in different ways. Our warm thanks are due to the Society of the Faith, who made the lectures possible.

As a former Lambeth Librarian, I may, perhaps, be allowed a personal remark on my own great pleasure at seeing this publication appear. It is a gauge of the enlightened policy which has directed this Library during its reconstruction after the last war. It is probably well known that the Library was then badly bombed and suffered considerable damage. Its rehabilitation was initiated by the perceptive and much appreciated help of the Pilgrim Trust, but the continuation of the great scheme for reorganization would never have been possible without the sustained and remarkable generosity of the Church Commissioners. To every appeal they responded with the utmost patience and good will. As a result of their interest, the Library was rehabilitated and greatly extended, and it was more firmly linked with academic circles than hitherto. Once the physical war damage to the buildings and books had been repaired, the Library could function again as an efficient unit, but attempts were also made by the Trustees and the Advisory Committee to make it, in a more vital sense, a centre of Church history and culture. As an example of this, the quatercentenary of Cranmer's death was celebrated in 1956 by a large exhibition and by a series of three lectures, which were inaugurated by the Archbishop of Canterbury and later published. These were so successful that this

present more ambitious course, covering almost the whole gamut
of the history of the English Church, was made possible. My own
hope is that Lambeth will continue to develop as a centre for
studies such as this; that it will be enabled in the future to
initiate other publications which will provide fresh interpreta-
tions of the history and culture of the English Church in all its
periods and aspects.

C. R. DODWELL

Trinity College
  Cambridge

CONTENTS

EDITOR'S PREFACE   page 5

THE ANGLO-SAXON PERIOD   9
Professor R. R. Darlington

THE TWELFTH AND THIRTEENTH
    CENTURIES   25
The Revd. Professor M. D. Knowles

THE LATER MIDDLE AGES   42
W. A. Pantin

THE SIXTEENTH CENTURY   60
The Revd. Professor Owen Chadwick

THE SEVENTEENTH AND
    EIGHTEENTH CENTURIES   73
The Very Revd. Norman Sykes

THE NINETEENTH AND TWENTIETH
    CENTURIES   95
The Revd. Canon H. M. Waddams

INDEX   120

1

THE ANGLO-SAXON PERIOD

Professor R. R. Darlington

THE period covered by this lecture, four and a half centuries and more, is roughly equal to that which separates the Norman Conquest from the Reformation, and likewise the Reformation from the present day. Though the materials for the study of Church history before the Norman Conquest are obviously far less abundant than for later periods of equal length, there is perhaps no age in which the phrase 'relations with the Continent' covers so much of the known history of the English Church as the early part of our period. Fortunately, few aspects of early English history have received fuller treatment from modern historians than the Conversion. It is equally fortunate that in his Ford Lectures entitled *England and the Continent in the Eighth Century* the late Wilhelm Levison, whose knowledge of Continental sources is never likely to be surpassed, covered in great detail almost all the aspects of the late seventh and eighth centuries which fall within the range of this lecture. No apology is needed therefore for the brevity of the comments offered here on subjects which are so well known to all scholars.

The unique position of the Anglo-Saxon Church as the offshoot of Rome, of which Englishmen were very conscious, coloured much of its later history. Augustine may not have achieved as much as Gregory had hoped, but a Church on the Roman model was founded by men who were sent from Rome and guided by the pope himself. From Gregory's own letters we derive the picture of him as a man who, amidst many other preoccupations, meditated upon the problems confronting his emissaries in a distant land, sent carefully considered answers to their inquiries and drew up a plan for the future organization of the Church which they were creating. The feeling of gratitude

9

to Rome which led Bede in a famous passage to describe Pope Gregory as the apostle of the English nation is reflected in the actions and writings of succeeding generations of Englishmen. By a piece of good fortune, the task of uniting the English Church after the Synod of Whitby and providing it with effective organization fell to a man chosen by Pope Vitalian. No Church outside Italy owed so much to Rome as the Anglo-Saxon, or was more closely linked with the papacy. At an early date Englishmen started making journeys to Rome, and during the archiepiscopate of Theodore of Tarsus visits and communications were more frequent than before. Wilfrid's opposition to Theodore gave rise to the earliest appeals to Rome and, in the time of Pope Agatho, Wilfrid and others secured the earliest papal privileges known to have been granted to English monasteries. The popes sent letters and envoys to England, and papal councils discussed the needs of the English Church.

It cannot be seriously questioned that the remarkable cultural development of England in the seventh and eighth centuries was for the most part the outcome of contact with the Continent. Though caution is desirable, it seems fairly safe to say that the origins of English sculpture and architecture are to be found on the Continent or farther afield rather than in Britain. The influence of Continental Europe and perhaps also the Near East can be traced alongside that of pagan England and Celtic Britain in the decorated manuscripts of the age. To Continental influence in the main may be attributed the remarkable level of English scholarship in Bede's age. English libraries were built up with books brought from Italy and Gaul, and nothing shows more clearly than the contents of these libraries, as reconstructed from the works of Bede and other scholars, that the English revival of learning was the unexpected product of the somewhat meagre intellectual activity of the fifth and sixth centuries on the Continent. The emergence in England of a group of scholars with a good knowledge of Greek as well as Latin is one of the most interesting results of the presence of Archbishop Theodore under whom, and Abbot Hadrian, the range of studies at Canterbury was exceptionally wide.

It is difficult to discover whether the Scottish missionaries, who undoubtedly played a large part in the conversion, made any considerable contribution to the growth of English scholarship, for there is little convincing evidence that Ireland had much to offer. To Ireland the English owed the handwriting known as insular script and probably also the regrettable literary fashion, the writing of 'Hisperic' Latin, of which Aldhelm was unfortunately the leading exponent. The wider claims which have often been made for Ireland do not appear to have been substantiated. It is equally difficult to assess the contribution of the Scots to the growth and character of English monasticism, for extreme asceticism was not peculiar to Ireland and, though the first foundations of this type in Northumbria are very early, the double monasteries of England were probably modelled on those of contemporary Gaul to which English men and still more English women betook themselves in the first half of the seventh century. Though it is impossible to prove the accepted view that the monastery of S. Peter and S. Paul at Canterbury was the first house outside Italy to follow the rule of S. Benedict, the rule was generally observed in England before the end of the seventh century, and in the eighth century English influence helped to popularize it on the Continent.

In consequence of the Roman origin of the Anglo-Saxon Church, English missionary activity, which sprang chiefly from consciousness of kinship with Germanic peoples who were still heathen, had far-reaching effects on the whole of Western Europe. In the regions where they worked, the English missionaries founded churches and monasteries to which English learning was transplanted together with books, and copies of books, which had earlier been brought from Italy. The contribution of English scholars in monasteries and at the Frankish court to the Carolingian Renaissance needs no further emphasis. Equally well known is the role of Boniface as the reformer and reorganizer of the Frankish Church. Gregory the Great's interest in a neglected people in a remote land brought rich rewards to the papacy in the eighth century. Willibrord and Boniface, consciously looking back to the days of Augustine, deliberately sought papal approval and guidance. Under the leadership of Boniface 'legatus Germanicus sedis apostolicae' the Anglo-Saxons gained for the pope power over the Frankish Church such as he had never before enjoyed. England appears to have played a considerable part in the evolution of the machinery by which in later times the papacy maintained control over the West. The theory that the powers of the metropolitan could be exercised only after the pallium had been received from the pope seems to have first emerged when Gregory the Great founded the English Church. The rule was observed in England from the seventh century and by the English on the Continent in the eighth. Further, Boniface appears not only to have made a profession of faith but also to have taken an oath of obedience to the pope. It seems clear that the English on the Continent disseminated ideas and practices which by degrees met with general acceptance. Not least significant among the usages which they took to the Continent was the practice of dating events by the era of the Incarnation which originated in England in Bede's age. From the great mass of surviving correspondence it is evident that English churchmen on the Continent kept in close touch with their homeland and that the English Church was the model which they strove to reproduce in hitherto heathen lands and regions where ecclesiastical life had decayed. Though quick to criticize what they considered to be faults, their general attitude was one of respect and humility towards the Church by which they had been reared. To a marked degree unity of purpose characterized the activities of the papacy, the English on the Continent and the prelates in England. Just before the middle of the century, for instance, Pope Zacharias wrote to both England and Germany urging measures of reform, and in 747 Archbishop Cuthbert in the synod of Clovesho promulgated canons which are closely related to those of a Frankish synod held by Boniface in the same year.

The habit of seeking papal approval and guidance was deeply rooted in the early English Church and on the whole papal intervention was beneficial, but more than one pope, making an important decision, seems to have been imperfectly acquainted with local conditions. It is significant that Archbishop Theodore ignored Agatho's decree ordering Wilfrid's restoration. The establishment of an archbishopric of York was, it is true, part of Gregory the Great's scheme, but the grant of the pallium to

Bishop Egbert in 735, in the words of Sir Frank Stenton, 'destroyed the constitutional unity of the English Church.' Later popes were not strikingly successful in their handling of the problems arising from the friction between the kings of Mercia and the archbishops of Canterbury which, during a period of about forty years, led to frequent recourse to Rome. Hadrian I was probably ill-advised to sanction the creation of the archbishopric of Lichfield and Leo III might have given more sympathetic consideration to the proposal, apparently made about ten years later, to abolish both Canterbury and Lichfield and revert to Gregory the Great's original plan to locate the seat of the southern archbishop at London. It is unfortunate that we know so little about the part played by the pope in the long and violent quarrel between Archbishop Wulfred and King Cenwulf of Mercia which broke out soon after the restoration to Canterbury of its ancient rights. This seems to be the only occasion in Anglo-Saxon history on which a king involved in conflict with the Archbishop of Canterbury appealed to Rome.

With the passing of political predominance over Kent from Mercia to Wessex in the time of Egbert the friction in which a series of archbishops had been involved came to an end. King Ethelwulf's approach to the pope took a more pleasant form than that of bringing accusations against an archbishop. Like two of his predecessors, Caedwalla and Ine, he was drawn to Rome by piety, though it was not his intention to end his days there. In 853 he sent his youngest son Alfred, a child of four, to Rome, and part of Pope Leo IV's letter telling the king how he had invested the infant with the insignia of a Roman consul has come down to us. Two years later Ethelwulf himself went to Rome and spent a year there. By a piece of good fortune this king had a Frankish secretary, Felix, who was a friend of Lupus, abbot of Ferrières. Among the letters of Lupus are two which he wrote, probably in 852, to the church of York when he was trying to borrow books from the famous library there. At the close of the eighth century English libraries and schools were in the opinion of Alcuin superior to those of the Franks, and the letters of Lupus show that at least one of the English centres of learning maintained its reputation to the middle of the ninth century. Charters and legal records of the early ninth century suggest that by that date scholarship had declined to a marked degree in Kent, but decay was not universal, and it seems that the disastrous phase when English scholars were reduced to a mere handful and Benedictine monasticism virtually disappeared was not reached until shortly before the accession of Alfred to the West Saxon throne.

In southern England the work of restoration and reform was begun even before the end of the ninth century. Though Alfred looked back to the age of Bede for inspiration and called to his court surviving scholars in Mercia and Wales, he eagerly sought help from abroad where some religious centres had partially escaped the disruption and decay which were almost universal at this time. To Fulk, archbishop of Rheims, was due the presence in England of Grimbald of S. Bertin's, who occupied a prominent place among the scholars who helped Alfred to make his English translations. Though in the tenth century interest tends to centre in the revival of monastic life, Alfred's objectives, above all the improvement of the standard of education among the lower clergy, were always kept in view. This is evident from the canons of Archbishop Oda, the pastoral activities of Dunstan, Oswald and other bishops, and the writings of Ælfric of Eynsham and Byrhtferth of Ramsey. Not least among the tasks unobtrusively accomplished by the English clergy in the early tenth century was the conversion to Christianity of the Scandinavians who had settled in eastern and northern England in the time of Alfred. Later, Englishmen worked among the Scandinavians of Norway and the remoter parts of Denmark and Sweden and, though their activities had no such spectacular consequences as those of Boniface and his contemporaries, their work was of permanent significance, and the later Norwegian Church possessed features which can be traced back to the English of the tenth and eleventh centuries.

In this period Scandinavia was greatly influenced by English civilization, and in England itself it is easy to trace the effects of contact with the Scandinavian peoples on contemporary art. English cultural development of the later Anglo-Saxon period owed much to Byzantium and Italy, but even more to the

Carolingian dominions. The architecture of the period is akin to the Carolingian Romanesque of the Rhineland. Carolingian influence contributed much to the revival of manuscript decoration among the English, whose work later had considerable effect on Continental art. The origin of the so-called Winchester style remains uncertain, but there can be no doubt that it is based on Carolingian manuscripts, of which many were brought to England in the first half of the tenth century, and, as Professor Wormald has observed, 'It is likely that several Carolingian schools made their contribution to it in one way and another.' Likewise we do not know from which centres on the Continent the Carolingian minuscule was introduced into England. The characteristic insular script was still widely used, but the Carolingian hand came to be regarded as more appropriate for Latin texts. As Mr. Ker has said in the introduction to his *Catalogue of Manuscripts containing Anglo-Saxon*, 'The scribes became accustomed to using two alphabets, one for Latin derived from the Caroline minuscule and one for the vernacular derived from Anglo-Saxon minuscule,' and the carefully trained scribe, writing a book in which Latin and Old English occurred together, wrote two scripts with equal skill. Most of the foreign churchmen who came to England in the tenth century and the first half of the eleventh came from various parts of the Carolingian dominions. In the first half of the tenth century a number of ecclesiastics whose names suggest that they were of German origin can be identified. In the latter half of the century monks came from the reformed houses of France and the Low Countries and there was a sprinkling of Germans such as the Saxon priest 'B' who wrote the earliest life of Dunstan. Lotharingians formed a significant element in the episcopate in the eleventh century, and Regenbald, the head of King Edward's scriptorium, was presumably of German extraction. Finally, the revival of canonical life among secular clerks was partly a native movement and in part the result of the close association with Lorraine.

Contacts with the Continent in the reigns of Alfred and Edward the Elder contributed little or nothing to the revival of Benedictine monasticism. Alfred went so far as to bring to England from 'Gaul' not only monks but also foreign children to be trained as monks, but episodes such as the attempted murder of John the Old Saxon by members of the Frankish community which Alfred established at Athelney, suggest that the unreformed houses across the Channel were poor recruiting grounds. There is no reason to suppose that the rule of S. Benedict was observed at the New Minster at Winchester which Edward the Elder entrusted to Grimbald. Athelstan was well known on the Continent as the benefactor of monasteries, but when in 929 Coenwald, bishop of Worcester, took the king's gifts to the monasteries *per totam Germaniam,* Cluniac influence was only just beginning to penetrate beyond Burgundy and Aquitaine, and the Lotharingian movement was in its early stages. About 930 Odo, abbot of Cluny, reformed Fleury, and the reform of Blandinium at Ghent was undertaken by Gerard of Brogne about seven years later. Archbishop Oda, who himself received the habit from Fleury, is the first English prelate to establish direct contact with a Continental centre of reform. To that house he sent his nephew Oswald, who appears to have been joined by other young Englishmen. Somewhat later, Ethelwold, after abandoning his plan to go abroad himself, sent to Fleury one of his monks at Abingdon named Osgar. Even more important was the association between England and Blandinium from the time of Dunstan's residence there during his exile. For about twelve years Dunstan had been the leader of a native movement which owed little or nothing to foreign example. His exile made him the 'first effective link between the revived English monasticism and the great Continental reforms.' Shortly after Dunstan's return, Oswald came back from Fleury, and the year 957–8 is the beginning of a new phase in which the English reform movement was to a marked degree influenced by the Continent.

From the lives of Dunstan, Ethelwold and Oswald, chronicles and letters, it is evident that in the reign of Edgar there was frequent intercourse between England and foreign houses, above all Fleury and Blandinium. The abbots of these two monasteries were invited to send representatives to the council of Winchester at which the *Regularis Concordia* was drawn up, and Abbot Womar of Blandinium is known to have visited England on either this or a later occasion. The detailed examination of the

Regularis Concordia, a skilful blending of native usages and foreign customs, has made it possible to assess the relative importance of the contributions of Fleury and Blandinium, for though the tenth-century customs of neither of these houses have come down to us, resemblances between the *Concordia* and Cluniac custom may reasonably be attributed to Fleury and parallels with the surviving customs of the Lotharingian monasteries to Blandinium. Dom Thomas Symons concludes that there is a 'higher proportion of agreement with Lotharingian than with Cluniac usage. In other words it looks as though the customs of Ghent . . . had specially commended themselves to the English.' The *Concordia* also shows that the English monastic leaders were influenced by the ideas of Benedict of Aniane on uniformity and the relations between the secular ruler and the monasteries in his dominions. Though it was not proposed that King Edgar should appoint inspectors to ensure uniformity of observance, it was clearly intended that the customs should be binding on all since 'the assembly as one man made a solemn vow . . . that, living all their life under the yoke of the Rule, they would carry out these selfsame monastic customs openly and with one uniform observance.' The *Regularis Concordia,* which remained the standard usage of English monasteries for a century, had been promulgated by royal and ecclesiastical authority in a synodical council and so had an official standing which was not enjoyed by Lanfranc's monastic constitutions, largely of Cluniac origin, by which it was superseded at Canterbury and other houses in the late eleventh century.

It is misleading to suggest that after the issue of the *Regularis Concordia* the English reformers lost contact with foreign houses. In the ensuing period reform spread to regions hitherto unaffected, such as Normandy, but there was no great new monastic movement on the Continent. The presence in England of foreign monks such as the distinguished scholar Abbo of Fleury, who resided for some time at Ramsey, the visits of English prelates to foreign houses such as S. Bertin's which was on the route to Rome, gifts such as those of Archbishop Aldulf of York to Fleury, the writing of a life of Dunstan by Adelard of Blandinium between 1006 and 1011, the survival of many letters

which Englishmen wrote to and received from foreign churchmen, and finally the evidence of manuscripts, constitute adequate
proof that established ties were maintained in the late tenth century and well into the eleventh. Mr. Grierson has observed that
the letters which passed between England and Flanders 'mention
casually the names of minor ecclesiastics who seem to have been
quite accustomed to travelling backwards and forwards between
the two countries, and allude to gifts made by Dunstan and his
successors to Flemish monasteries.' The settlement in England of
two monks of S. Bertin's, who distinguished themselves as writers
of saints' lives, Folcard and Goscelin, shows that the connection
with this house was maintained to the eve of the Conquest.
Contact with more distant places is reflected in the presence in
England of Baldwin, a monk of S. Denis at Paris, and Abbot
Wulfric's plan to build at S. Augustine's, Canterbury, a church
resembling one built earlier in the century at Dijon.

The building of King Edward's new abbey at Westminster on
the model of Jumièges is the obvious consequence of the king's
Norman upbringing and the presence of the monk Robert, suc-
cessively Bishop of London and Archbishop of Canterbury, but
otherwise the effects of contact with the recently founded or
reformed monasteries of the duchy are difficult to assess. The
distinctive qualities of Norman monasticism, above all its intellectual vigour, which enabled it to make so significant a contribution after the Conquest, seem to date from a comparatively late
phase when Lanfranc's influence was widely felt in the duchy.
Three of the half dozen foreign churches holding land in England
in 1066 were Norman: the monastery of Holy Trinity at Fécamp,
which already possessed nearly all the property it had in 1086
when its estates exceeded in value those of any other foreign
church, the monastery of S. Audoen or Ouen of Rouen, and the
cathedral church of Rouen which had been given a valuable
estate by the English earl, Odda, probably in 1051 or 1052. It is
just possible that S. Denis at Paris was the first foreign monastery
to acquire land in England, since genuine grants of the late eighth
and ninth centuries may lie behind the forged charters attributed
to King Offa and other Englishmen, but the property which
S. Denis had in England in 1066 was recently acquired, probably

through the monk Baldwin who was the king's physician. S. Remigius of Rheims had acquired its English possessions not long before the Conquest by the gift of Earl Ælfgar, whose son, Burgheard, is said to have died and been buried at Rheims on the way back from Rome (1061 or 1062). Blandinium seems to have first acquired land in England in the tenth century, though it is not agreed whether the original gift of Lewisham was made by King Edgar or by King Alfred's daughter, Ælfthryth, who married Baldwin II, count of Flanders.

The Scandinavian wars of King Alfred's time had little effect on relations between England and Rome. Pilgrims of royal birth and other laymen and ecclesiastics continued to make their way to the holy city. Portions of letters of Pope John VIII written between 873 and 875 to King Burgred of Mercia and to the Archbishops of Canterbury and York have come down to us. The pope would appear to have been unaware of the gravity of the political situation, for he is found writing about rather common-place moral evils such as the seduction of nuns in his letter to King Burgred, who was then about to abandon his kingdom and go to Rome. To the archbishops he wrote about the adoption of clerical garments of Roman fashion, though both prelates must have been facing graver issues than the wearing of ankle-length tunics. The pope says that he has assembled the leading English-men living 'near the blessed apostle Peter' and that they have agreed to substitute the clerical for the lay habit. Some of these Englishmen were presumably those who belonged to the Saxon 'school' or quarter at Rome, an ancient institution to which we have several references in the late ninth century. More interesting is Pope John's reply to a letter of Archbishop Ethelred (about 878) in which he says 'in accordance with the custom of your predecessors you seek both to refer the necessary concerns of your Church to our episcopate as to its teacher and to receive from the apostolic see . . . the advice and support of authority con-cerning certain adversities which it is suffering.' The letter goes on to make obscure criticisms of King Alfred, whose relations with the papacy in other respects were most cordial. Pope Marinus, who died in 884, sent him gifts, and at his request freed the Saxon 'school' from taxation. Of greater significance are the references to the taking of the alms of the West Saxon people and their king to Rome in the reigns of Alfred and Edward the Elder. It is recorded in the Anglo-Saxon Chronicle that in 887 and 888 the alms of King Alfred and the West Saxon people were taken to Rome by an ealdorman, that in 889 there was no such formal deputation, though the king sent letters by messengers, and that in 890 the alms of the West Saxons and their king were taken by an abbot. Similarly Archbishop Plegmund is said to have taken the alms of the West Saxons and King Edward the Elder with him when he went to Rome. In these gifts, which differ from the donations of King Offa and King Ethelwulf since they appear to be payments by a people and their king, lies probably the origin of Peter's Pence. Payment under penalty of excommunication is enjoined on all men by one of the decrees of the synod which met in London under Archbishops Oda and Wulfstan with the co-operation of King Edmund about 945, and in the laws of Edgar, Ethelred and Cnut, which were binding on the whole of England the penalties for non-payment are ruinous. Edgar's second code enjoins that any one who does not pay his hearthpenny on S. Peter's day shall take it to Rome together with 30 pence more and on his return with proof that he has handed the money over, he is to pay 120 shillings to the king. If he refuses, he must go to Rome and on his return pay 200 shillings, and if he fails a third time to obey he forfeits everything. In the laws of Ethelred and Cnut the penalty is lighter, but still sufficient to ruin many men—30 pence together with the penny withheld to the Church, and 120 shillings to the king. It would be unwise to regard Edgar's order sending the offender to Rome as impracticable. One of Ethelred's laws, repeated in Cnut's second code, requires a priest guilty of homicide or other serious crime to travel as a pilgrim as far as the pope shall appoint, and such a priest presumably had to go to Rome in person. The inclusion of a group of documents which purport to be papal letters of the late tenth and early eleventh centuries in an English canonical collection seems to imply that it was the custom for persons who had killed their kinsmen by accident to go to Rome so that suitable penance might be imposed by the pope.

There has come down to us also a letter addressed by Pope

Formosus to the English bishops between 891 and 896 which appears to refer to the disruption of the ecclesiastical organization by the Danish wars but might easily be read as a demand for more bishoprics. The pope seems to urge them to make greater efforts to convert the heathen Danes and tells them not to allow 'the flock of God to wander and be scattered and dispersed for lack of pastors.' In the passage stating that when *quilibet sacerdotum* dies another should be substituted without delay and as soon as the archbishop is informed of his brother's death, another should after canonical election be consecrated to succeed the deceased, *sacerdos* seems to mean bishop. The letter may help to explain why before the end of the tenth century the view was current that a letter written by Formosus to Edward the Elder, who did not become king until three years after this pope's death, led directly to the multiplication of the West Saxon sees about 909. On the other hand, the episode is very obscure, and since Archbishop Plegmund visited Rome in 908, it would be unwise to rule out the possibility that the first phase of diocesan reorganization in the tenth century owed something to papal interest in English affairs.

It has been suggested that Plegmund went to Rome because the validity of his own position was affected by the condemnation of Formosus and that he needed to secure from Sergius III confirmation and recognition of the pallium which (according to a late tradition) Formosus had granted to him. It is possible that the practice whereby the archbishops of Canterbury went to Rome in person to obtain the pallium is in some way connected with this episode. Neither of the vigorous ninth century popes Nicholas I and John VIII appears to have insisted on a personal visit by the metropolitan, and as late as 877 John VIII decreed that all metropolitans should send to Rome for it within three years of their election. Personal visits by continental metropolitans are exceptional, whereas the archbishops of Canterbury regularly went to Rome from 927 and the archbishops of York from 1026. Though the journey to and from Rome was commonly undertaken by English churchmen, it could be dangerous as the fate of Dunstan's predecessor Ælfsige, who was frozen to death in the Alps, shows. Incidental notices sometimes give a clue to the route followed, and the itinerary of Archbishop Sigeric giving the names of about eighty places through which he passed on his journey from Rome to the English Channel in 990 has come down to us. Since the burdensome journey seems to have been the subject of an English protest to the pope about 1000, and Cnut in 1027 was driven to complain about the excessive sums demanded of the archbishops by the pope, it may seem improbable the practice originated with the English prelates, yet it is difficult to suggest a pope of the period 877 to 927, other than Sergius III, who is likely to have insisted on a personal visit by the Archbishop of Canterbury. The existence of this practice among the English long before it became established on the Continent may have contributed to the general acquiescence in the demands of the reformed papacy, just as Peter's Pence, still paid regularly on the eve of the Conquest, could be represented as tribute to Rome.

It can be said that the relations between England and Rome were at least as close as could be expected in the long period when papal authority was only spasmodically asserted and the initiative seldom rested with Rome. The more abundant evidence of papal intervention in English affairs in the reign of Edward the Confessor is the direct consequence of the assumption by Pope Leo IX of leadership of the reform movement. King Edward at once showed himself ready to co-operate with the reformed papacy and no attempt was made before the Conquest to place limitations on papal activities. When Leo held his great synod at Rheims in 1049 a bishop and two abbots were sent 'so that they might inform the king of whatever was decided there,' and this was presumably one of the functions of English prelates who attended other councils. Pope Leo was consulted by Bishop Leofric before he transferred his see from Crediton to Exeter, and Archbishop Robert's refusal to consecrate the abbot of Abingdon to the see of London even though he presented himself with the king's writ, may have been an attempt to enforce Leo's decree at Rheims that no one should undertake the government of a church unless he had been elected by the clergy and people. Though King Edgar secured papal approval of the replacement of clerks by monks at Winchester Cathedral, the Old

Minster, and at least one house appealed to the pope against an aggressive ealdorman, the English monasteries reformed in the tenth century had rarely sought papal privileges, probably because the friendship of the king and of the episcopate rendered them unnecessary. The reformed papacy encouraged monasteries and other churches to seek its protection, and the type of privilege obtained by Chertsey Abbey from Leo's successor Victor II, safeguarding it in the possession of its property, was to become very common in England. The privilege brought back from Rome in April 1061 by Giso, bishop of Wells, which still survives, is a confirmation of the same type, but the one which Nicholas II granted a few days later, on 5 May, to Wulfwig, bishop of Dorchester, is more significant, for by its terms the pope settled in Wulfwig's favour a dispute which had arisen between the bishops of Dorchester and the archbishops of York. The view that Ealdred was the archbishop who made the encroachments of which Wulfwig complained seems to involve the improbable assumptions that immediately after his appointment on 25 December 1060 Ealdred seized the diocese of Lindsey, which appears to have become extinct in the early eleventh century, and certain properties of the bishop of Dorchester, and that Wulfwig appealed to Rome with great promptitude without trying to get redress in England. It is however possible that Alvric of the bull is Archbishop Ælfric, who was in office from 1023 to 1051, and that the death of Archbishop Cynesige in December 1060, precipitated Wulfwig's appeal. When Ealdred went to Rome in 1061, Nicholas II again asserted papal authority by refusing him the pallium until he had agreed to surrender the bishopric of Worcester, and by deciding to send legates to England. The two legates, who must have left Rome after the election of Alexander II, spent Lent 1062 at Worcester, and at the Easter court proposed that Wulfstan, then prior, should be chosen bishop of Worcester in Ealdred's stead.

The view that the late Old English Church was isolated and decadent may now be regarded as discredited. During the latter part of the Confessor's reign, however, the unfortunate events of 1052 cast a shadow over relations with Rome. When Archbishop Robert fled along with Ulf, the Norman bishop of Dorchester, they were considered to have abandoned their sees, both of which were treated as vacant, and Stigand, bishop of Winchester, was forthwith given the archbishopric. The case against Stigand, as seen by the stricter English clergy, is stated in Bishop Wulfstan's profession of obedience to Lanfranc. Stigand, says Wulfstan, because he had invaded the see of Canterbury and used the rightful occupant's pallium, had been summoned, excommunicated and condemned by Popes Leo, Victor, Stephen, Nicholas and Alexander. It is surprising that the Conqueror allowed a man who could be regarded as 'excommunicated' to consecrate the first bishop whom he appointed in England, Remigius of Dorchester, but the removal of Stigand was not a matter of importance to the Normans as it was to the papacy. The pope's acceptance of Wulfwig of Dorchester, who was certainly appointed while Ulf was still alive, suggests that in the eyes of Rome Stigand's gravest offence was his association with Pope Benedict X. In England, the validity of the election of Pope Benedict from whom, during the nine months when he was undisputed pope, Stigand obtained his own pallium, does not seem to have been questioned until the party of reform elected Nicholas II who was immediately recognized by the English Church. Stigand's position was thereafter regarded as uncanonical. Bishops avoided consecration by him and the prelates of the southern province felt unable to make the customary profession of obedience to their metropolitan. It was a singular misfortune that the Church which had been founded, organized and nurtured by the papacy, and in its turn had played a considerable part in extending papal authority on the Continent should have had as its principal ecclesiastic in 1066 a man whom the pope desired to remove from office. Regrettable though it is on moral grounds, there seems to be no doubt that Alexander gave open support to Duke William in his plans for war against England. Thus it came about that the successor of the apostle of the English nation was instrumental in the destruction of the Church which had made no small contribution to the cultural and religious life of Western Europe, and had a unique record of devotion to Rome.

2

THE TWELFTH AND THIRTEENTH
CENTURIES

Professor M. D. Knowles

THE immediate and also the lasting result of the Norman Conquest was that it made England culturally and socially an integral part of Western Europe. For the two following centuries the English Channel ceased to be a barrier or a moat and shrank to the significance of a large lake or river. For more than a century the kings of England were dukes of Normandy, and for almost two centuries the king of England was the effective overlord of various provinces of what is now France. Moreover, landholders of all kinds, royal, ecclesiastical and private, held estates on either side of the Channel, and kings and administrators went incessantly backwards and forwards on their lawful occasions, speaking the same language wherever they went and guiding similar institutions. This close political and social connection with Europe in a somewhat different form is so much a part of all our lives and of all our modern history that it is easy to be unaware, or to forget, that but for the Norman Conquest it might have been long delayed or rendered less strong. In the early months of 1066 it seemed more likely that England's existing links with the Continent would be cut, and that she would become politically and socially a part of the Scandinavian world. Had there been a Danish rather than a Norman Conquest, England not only might have remained for long or for ever outside *Latinitas,* the European civilization of the Middle Ages, but she and her Scandinavian relations might have passed right through the medieval centuries as a different civilization altogether.

This political and social and cultural *Anschluss,* however, important as it was in itself, was rendered infinitely more significant by the circumstances of the age in which it occurred. In that eleventh century took place two great movements, two great renaissances, the one on a deep and fundamental level of mental life, the other on a most important level of religious government and organization. The first was that great intellectual awakening which has been called by many names, but which was in essence the attainment of adolescence and manhood by a new civilization, namely that of medieval Western Europe, the second, ultimately dependent upon the first as its basic impulse, was the great spiritual revival of the age, of which the two most striking external manifestations were the multiplication and diffusion of various forms of the monastic life and the revival of the papacy as a dynamic and expanding force.

Taken together, these new agencies, which transcended all minor differences of time and place and race, were able to create, in the wider area of Western Europe, a single comprehensive intellectual climate that was distinctive enough to assimilate or to bear down, at least on the higher, articulate levels, all local or regional differences and varieties, while in the purely ecclesiastical sphere there evolved a single comprehensive administrative system directed by a single theological and legal idea, that of unity imposing order. For three hundred years, from 1050 to 1350, North-western Europe from the Straits of Messina to the Firth of Forth, and from the marshes of Poland to those of Islamic Spain, was a single undifferentiated religious and cultural bloc speaking a single learned language for all purposes of instruction and administration and devotion, governed ecclesiastically by a single network of government and a single body of law, a vast area within which all men of education could circulate freely and find a master, an audience and a career.

Let us take these various renaissances, and see how each affected the Church in this country, and trace the influence that crossed and recrossed the Channel in consequence.

In the religious sphere, with which alone we are concerned at present, the change was least noticeable on the theological and devotional level. England, at least since the days of Theodore and Bede, if not also since those of Augustine, had drawn its methods and inspirations directly from the Continent, in different degrees and at different times. Always and everywhere between the age of S. Benedict and that of Lanfranc Englishmen in days of peace and happiness had looked to the past in Mediterranean lands for masters, for exemplars and for doctrine. But the commerce that had previously been spasmodic and fitful became, after the Norman Conquest, universal and constant. With the Normans began a steady stream of learning, as theologians and diffusers of all kinds of religious art and knowledge began to cross the Channel. For almost a century an overwhelming majority of the most celebrated bishops and abbots and divines and spiritual writers came from the Continent, and among them were some of the greatest names of the age; the theologians Lanfranc and Anselm, the lawyer Vacarius, bishops such as Osmund of Salisbury, William of S. Carilef of Durham, Gundulf of Rochester, and later Henry of Winchester, Theobald of Canterbury and Hugh of Lincoln, with abbots such as Gilbert Crispin of Westminster, Faricius of Abingdon, and William of Rievaulx.

Along with the masters came the methods and techniques. Lanfranc and Anselm were in their different ways the two greatest teachers of their generation, and Anselm was an original thinker of the very highest rank, but neither had opportunity when in England to form a school. It was on a lower and less spectacular level, in the monastic cloister, and later in the cathedral schools of Exeter, Lincoln and Salisbury, and in the household of archbishops of Canterbury, that the continental methods were applied and diffused. England, however, never had episcopal schools to rival Chartres, Laon, Sens and the rest; it is noteworthy that while almost all the continental universities north of the Alps sprang from cathedral schools neither Oxford nor Cambridge had any connection with one. Indeed in the first half of the twelfth century the monasteries were still the hearths of learning; in this respect, as in so many others, there was a time-lag of half a century between England and the rest of Western Europe. During this half-century, and far beyond it, most of the promising young clerks of England went to France or Italy for all schooling beyond grammar—that is, normally, to Paris or to Bologna. John of Salisbury is one of the first, as he is certainly one of the most celebrated of these, but a host of his countrymen, including in his day Thomas Becket of London, took the same road, and the Channel craft never lacked for passengers in either direction. John, indeed, after making his career in France and Italy, as well as at Canterbury, ended his days as Bishop of Chartres, but many scholars returned to live and to die in their native land. Thus Robert, called of Melun from his first home of fame, became a Paris master of the first rank and returned home at last to be Bishop of Hereford, as did Hilary, who presumably went to Bologna before serving in the papal curia and returning to be Bishop of Chichester. Others, remaining abroad, nevertheless helped to strengthen the bonds between their new home and their old, as did Adam of the Petit Pont at Paris and Robert Pullen who, after teaching at Paris and Oxford, became the first English cardinal and a patron of several of his countrymen, and Nicholas Brakespeare, the first and only English pope, who organized the Scandinavian Church on the Roman model as papal legate before his elevation to the chair of Peter, in which he took a special interest in the affairs of these islands.

The second great wave of continental influence came to England directly through the agency of the religious orders. This was indeed the first in time of all waves to make its presence felt as a massive force. It may seem almost paradoxical to say that monasticism, an institution which the West imported from the East, and which had never crossed mountains or seas save by means of a Rule or of persons vowed to a Rule, was in pre-Norman England a home product, but it is nevertheless true that the monastic revival of the tenth century had owed little or nothing directly to foreign monks and only a little to foreign monasteries. The abbeys had been founded by Englishmen and depended upon no superior overseas. The Rule, indeed, and most of the liturgical and disciplinary regulations, derived ultimately from ancient or Carolingian sources, but the heritage had long been common property of all Western Europe and was regarded as a part of the order of things throughout Western Christendom, almost as was the sacred liturgy itself. Now, however, there was a change. The first snowflakes were already in the air in the latter years of Edward the Confessor, when Deerhurst was given to S. Denis, and one or two Norman abbeys acquired churches or small estates in England, but the steady fall only began in the reign of the Conquoror and did not become a blizzard for sixty years.

The first change was the 'occupation' of most of the Old English abbeys by Norman abbots, the counterpart of the occupation of the Old English estates and episcopal sees by Duke William's men. This was a gradual process, following the incidence of voidances caused by death, flight, rebellion and deprivation, but it was fairly complete by the Conqueror's death. For our purposes, it is not primarily the Norman abbots in person that interest us, but the fact that they reformed or at least reinvigorated English monasticism with the transfusion of virile foreign blood, the discipline, the architecture, the monastic culture and art of Normandy. As a result, all save the smallest and most remote upland monasteries became Anglo-Norman in population and characteristics.

Secondly, there was the acquisition by gift of churches and small properties all over England by Norman and more distant continental monasteries, who thus gained a *pied-à-terre* in England which might be exploited or not in the future, but which implied the presence in England of numerous Norman or French religious engaged in the business of administration.

Thirdly, there was the foundation of new abbeys with monks drawn from overseas, such as Chester, a daughter of Bec, Battle, a foundation of Marmoutier and, most significant of all, Lewes from La Charitè-sur-Loire, with a monk of Cluny as its prior. This last, which introduced into England for the first time the 'order' which for almost a century had been spreading far and wide, is of particular interest, for the mother-house as well as the venerable matriarchal abbey were both well outside the Conqueror's duchy. It was the first sign, if we may continue our metaphor, that the snowfall was going to be heavy beyond all precedent.

Hitherto the new-comers from abroad had been representatives of old institutes and all, as traditional Benedictines, were near relatives of the Old English monasteries. What followed in the reign of Henry I and Stephen was on the contrary without precedent; the arrival and rapid multiplication in England of new monastic and canonical bodies which had not only originated abroad, but which were to a greater or lesser extent centred

upon a continental head house and directed from abroad by a
foreign or at least by an international governing body. Savigny,
Tiron, and above all Cîteaux, and in the next generation
Prémontré, Fontevrault, Grandmont and the Grande Charteuse,
all sent colonies scattered throughout the length and breadth of
England. Of these, the Cistercians and Premonstratensians
flourished and multiplied beyond all others. Throughout our
period this implied a constant flow of men and ideas across the
Channel; of abbots yearly going up to Cîteaux or Prémontré, of
'visitors' from abroad coming to England, of suitors and messengers and the conveyance of obit-rolls and books. Moreover the
new orders sent to England much besides the persons of their
founders. Forms and fashions of art, architecture and learning,
and the still more important traffic of ideas and spiritual ideals
came in battalions—among them the massive and magnetic
influence of Bernard, which gave a new direction and a new
urgency to so many aspects of doctrine and devotion. English
Cistercians were soon hard at it building abbeys on the model
of Pontigny and Fontenay and writing sermons on the Canticle
and devotional pieces in a style and manner almost indistinguishable from that of the Abbot of Clairvaux. Ailred's tractate
De spirituali amicitia and the hymn *Dulcis Jesu memoria* have
both been claimed as Bernard's, and neither would have been
written had he never existed, but the latter as well as the former
has recently been vindicated for an English author, though as
yet his name is unknown.

Something has been said in a previous lecture of the doctrinal
and disciplinary links between this country and the Continent in
the Old English period. A word will be said of discipline later;
here we may only note that as regards belief and devotion there
is, throughout our two centuries, nothing to be said, for throughout this period England continued to be in absolute solidarity in
every respect with the rest of Western Christendom. The new
external manifestations of devotion to our Lady which found
expression in the Lady Chapel, the Lady Mass and the Little
Office of our Lady, and the external cultus of the Blessed Sacrament and the popular manifestations of devotion to the Passion
and to the Sorrows of Mary spread rapidly to England, whatever

their source north or south of the Alps. The new doctrinal precisions and opinions, such as those of Transubstantiation and the Immaculate Conception, were taught or debated in exactly the same way as in Paris or Italy; English Cistercians, true to S. Bernard, opposed the introduction of the feast of the Conception which English black monks had done much to popularize, just as, a century or more later, English Dominicans opposed the doctrinal basis of the liturgical celebration when English Franciscans proposed it.

We now come, at long last, to what many would regard as the most salient feature of the age in Church history: the development of papal claims and activity. Here again the reign of the Conqueror coincided almost exactly with the decades in which Hildebrand, before and after his elevation to the papacy as Gregory VII, brought into the forefront of European interests the claims and demands of the reformed papacy in the realms of theological and political doctrine, of judicial competence, of legislation and of disciplinary control. Here again we have already been told how things stood in the Old English Church. While the paramountcy of the Roman Church as the centre of Christendom, the shrine of the Apostles and the goal of pilgrimage had been recognized, and the position of the Pope, the Vicar of Peter, as ultimate norm of the faith and source of authority had been accepted without question, the English Church, in the centuries since Charlemagne when Rome for long periods lost consciousness, at least in practical action, of her own dignity, had taken on an appearance of self-sufficiency and of nationalism without exact parallel in the West. The tradition of anointed kingship, the pervasive private ownership of churches, and the unique intermingling of churchmen and laymen in all great affairs, civil and ecclesiastical, gave the impression of a body standing very loosely to any higher control, and to any one lacking the sense of change and development of sentiments and institutions, the pre-Conquest Church might seem, as it seemed to Tudor propagandists, to differ little in spirit from the later Henrician establishment.

Duke William, for his part, had grown to manhood in Normandy in the midst of an ecclesiastical regime different indeed from this, but not incompatible with it. Though nearer to pagan brutality, and less gifted in spiritual and artistic matters than both Anglo-Saxon and French, the Normans had a drive and an efficiency without equal in the West, and also, in a way that might seem surprising, had become energetic supporters of the Church. For more than half a century the dukes had been fitfully but forcibly reformers. The monasteries of Normandy were, in the decades before the Conquest, more virile and observant as a group than those in either France or England. The Church itself had become a typical *Landeskirche* controlled by the duke. At some time before *c.* 1050 it had been drawn into the tightly woven feudal system, and bishops and abbots were tenants-inchief holding by military service. Bishops and abbots, often relatives of the ducal or baronial houses, were appointed or at least confirmed by the duke. The whole organization was defended against interference by jealous control. Yet it was a part of the Conqueror's greatness, and a feature of his character that differentiated him sharply from his descendants in the near future who were to claim him as their exemplar, that his desire for religious reform and well-being was sincere and his conception of its essence just, and that he regarded his surveillance as a duty and not merely as a pretext for aggrandizement or exploitation. He was a genuine reformer, even if, in Sir Frank Stenton's words 'he regarded himself not as the pope's minister, but as his collaborator and ally.'

All this, the personal control, the feudalized church, and the reforming spirit, came over to England with the Conqueror. William was in no wise anti-papal, but his conception of the papacy was that of the men of his youth. He sailed under the papal banner, and used papal legates in his first years in England for the reorganization of the dioceses and for the elimination of irregular or obnoxious bishops. The papacy he knew, however, was the papacy of twenty years earlier; he had not kept up with the change of outlook and had no thought of doing so. The English Church would be a *Landeskirche* under his control. In this he had neither hostility to Rome nor any desire for separatism, and he showed this by choosing, first as abbot for his new monastery at Caen, and later as his new archbishop, the trained

Lombard lawyer, later the most celebrated master of theology in Europe and the teacher of Christendom, Lanfranc. Lanfranc, like William, was a reformer; he was no anti-papalist; he counted cardinals and at least one pope, Alexander II, among his pupils; he accepted William's commission only at the direct command of the pope, and endeavoured vainly to resign his charge into the pope's hands within a few months, but like his king, he was a length behind the Roman vanguard. He had left Italy before the great days of Humbert and Hildebrand, and his conception of a reformed Church was a group of large provinces each controlled by an archbishop-primate. From the beginning he made it clear that the whole country was his concern, monks as well as clergy, and as he felt himself stronger he extended his grasp to include not only the province of York and the dioceses of Wales, but south-eastern Scotland and Ireland as far as he could reach.

At the same time he supported the Conqueror in his policy of independence, and as the years went on the king hardened in his outlook. It may have been a reaction, conscious or not, to the unfamiliar claims to dominion of the reformers, and possibly to that of feudal fealty that Gregory VII was making. The age was moving onwards, and popes and kings were adopting positions which to both Edward the Confessor and the pre-Leonine pontiffs would have seemed inconceivable. Within the ring-fence of the Conqueror's kingdom Lanfranc was given a free rein, and it is no exaggeration to say that he left a deeper mark upon the Church in England than did any archbishop between Theodore and Cranmer. Part of his work was directed towards a moral and spiritual revival such as any noteworthy bishop might have desired, but the external and permanent achievement of his pontificate was something quite unique. It was, if I may quote again the words of Sir Frank Stenton, not only for the sake of his authority, but by reason of their intrinsic truth, 'the prelude to a revolution, [for] it opened the Church at once to the full impact of foreign influences.' Lanfranc may not have been a Gregorian in Church politics, but he was undoubtedly a Gregorian as reformer. By his series of national councils, by his introduction of cathedral chapters, regular and secular, with all the continental organization, and by the multiplication of territorial archdeaconries he knit the English Church into an organic whole, with its nerve-centre at Canterbury. Above all, he was responsible for a measure of which even the Conqueror's perspicacity failed to see the consequences. Hitherto there had been no ecclesiastical courts in England; spiritual pleas had been heard at the hundred court, of which the bishop was often president, while spiritual matter of national importance came before the Witan. Whether the Conqueror's writ directing that spiritual causes should be dealt with by the bishop in accordance with the canons was intended merely as a piece of administrative tidying-up, or whether it was a matter of principle to Lanfranc is debatable; in the event it proved to be a landmark in English Church history. Church courts applied canon law, and canon law had thus fair entry into England at a moment doubly crucial, the moment when it was to spring up from a bush into a great tree, and the moment when it was to develop from being a general directory of Church discipline into a potent instrument of high policy and papal propaganda. A Cambridge scholar thirty years ago showed that Lanfranc himself had a large share in introducing the law books into England, and in editing them to suit the political climate of William's Church. Thenceforward, slowly at first, but with gathering momentum, canon law and the decrees of councils and papal letters that continually increased its volume and its relevance, reached far beyond its original application in courts Christian and became the *vis vivida* by which the organs of the Church functioned, and finally an arsenal and a fortress from which the Church could contain and even repulse the rulers of the world. From this small beginning, and despite the opposition, now clumsy, now intelligent, of the Conqueror's sons and descendants, and although the full Gregorian claims were in the end compromised, the machinery of a Church centralized upon the papacy took a firm hold in England. Canon law and the recognition of the Roman curia as the ultimate court of appeal in all suits, and of the papacy as a living fount of law and the ready oracle to every query became more and more familiar, and this, not only and not even principally through papal claims and acts of power, but through the daily traffic of privileges, elections and queries. In the second half of the century, moreover, under an unusually able and energetic group of bishops, and inaugurated by the hard times of the anarchy of Stephen's reign, the Becket controversy, and a series of *causes célèbres,* the intercourse between England and the Curia was constant and fruitful in legal pronouncements, while several of the English canonists led the world in the collection and codification of papal decretal letters. Indeed, at the turn of the century, when Innocent III had the whole of England, Church and State, on his hands, when the Canterbury and Evesham cases were still making legal history, and when Gerald of Wales was denouncing his colleagues and enemies at Rome, there must have been some, in Rome as well as in England, who felt that the connection of the English Church with the Continent had reached or passed the tolerable limit of closeness.

Canon law, rendered viable by Gratian, and the gradual emergence even in England of bishops trained in the schools and courts of the Continent, slowly transformed ecclesiastical procedure. Papal legates made their appearance and held councils; chapters and archbishops strove for canonical elections; monasteries, previously immune from disturbance at the hands of the diocesan in virtue of some ancient immunity or the status of royal *eigenkirche* or chapel, were assailed by the diocesan and sought papal protection and exemption. All this implied a vast increase of litigation, both criminal and contentious. Overwhelmed with causes great and small in which all the relevant facts and witnesses were local the Curia, between 1150 and 1200, took to employing, for all minor and some major pleas, the ancient resource of delegation to local or regional judges, usually three in number, chosen from among the ecclesiastical dignitaries or notabilities of the province.

In fine, as the twelfth century went on its course the whole machinery of the Gregorian papacy was deployed in England. Historians with varying themes to develop have stressed both the ubiquity of papal activity and the very real limitation imposed upon its exercise in England by conservative kings and administrators, by brute obstruction, and by the fundamental irregularity of all medieval practice, but when all reserves have been made the result is impressive enough. The legateships, though not the most successful instruments of papal policy in England, were sufficiently numerous even before 1200 to fill the pages of a recent monograph. The criterion of exemption came to be the *nullo mediante* clause which declared the immediate dependence of the house upon the Apostolic See, and the papal drive against lay control of prelacies, though unsuccessful on the feudal level, succeeded, when free election rather than investiture was the issue, in bringing to papal cognizance all disputed elections. Any one who has glanced through the records of one of the great law-suits of the age, such as that of the York election of the mid-century, or the controversy between Baldwin and the Canterbury monks, or who has followed the career of a curialist or canonist bishop such as Hilary of Chichester or Bartholomew of Exeter, will appreciate the great change that had taken place since the days of Lanfranc. The weakness of governance in Stephen's reign opened the door still wider, and for a run of years the ambitious and strongly papalist legate Henry of Winchester dominated the scene. Twenty years later, the long controversy between Henry II and Archbishop Thomas was a matter of European significance and its *dénouement* had the double result of removing hindrances to appeals to Rome and making of Canterbury one of the half-dozen major shrines of Christendom. It is not, indeed, to the high political issues or to the papal claims to dominion in the temporal sphere that we should look for the commerce between England and the Continent, but to the routine traffic between the Curia and England, which was now taken for granted as a normal and essential part of Church life.

The pontificate of Innocent III is universally recognized as a watershed in the history of the English Church. That great pope's achievement in reorganizing and reforming the disciplinary and sacramental life of the Church marked an epoch and influenced the future even more deeply than did his high claims to direct and control the political life of Europe and his intimate embroilment in English affairs. Yet if a new age dawned, an old age passed away. Up till 1198 the English Church for more than a century had been steadily remodelling itself after the pattern that a reformed papacy and an intellectual and canonical renaissance had made standard for Western Europe. In that process English-

men at home and abroad had taken their full share as teachers
and coadjutors, and on the levels of normal life and administration the process of change had been on the whole a voluntary
one, for all Churchmen of whatever country recognized that on
the balance a closer control from Rome had helped to speed the
cause of reform, of justice and of efficiency. The Curia itself,
with all its inevitable faults of tergiversation and venality, had on
the whole served the interests of the Church, rather than its own
private ends.

From 1216 onwards a new era began. The great Council of
the Lateran had codified and given legal sanction to traditional
discipline and by so doing had given a framework for parochial
and pastoral activity which the new generation of enlightened
university-trained bishops was able to use, but on the other hand
the creative, formative period of the medieval papacy had ended,
administration and justice became rigid and mechanical, and the
tendency on the part of the whole Curia to exploit the rest of
Christendom and to regard itself as the most precious part of the
Church grew steadily. Though the connection with the Continent and with Rome was as close as ever, the time had passed
when the external influence of the papacy upon the administration of the Church in England was genial and creative.

The creative age in the Church in general was, however, not
yet past. In the decade after the death of Innocent III the Continent released upon England its last great wave of religious
invasion, that of the friars. It was they who, in their first half-
century of fervour, did so much to cover the great hiatus in the
medieval organization of the Church—the lack of a regular
training for the rank and file of the clergy—by their apostolate
to the poorer classes of town and village folk, and by their
superior training both in dogmatic and moral theology and in the
art of popular preaching. They brought also to England devotions that remained popular till the Reformation and still abide
in the Church, such as the Christmas crib, the Stations of the
Cross and the use of the rosary beads.

There was also in the thirteenth century a connection with the
Continent new in the degree of its strength and influence, if not
precisely new in essence. This was the give-and-take of learning
across the Channel in the golden age of scholasticism.

The friars, first the Dominicans and Franciscans, then the Carmelites, Austin Hermits and the shortlived splinter groups, swept over England much in the same way as their predecessors, the white monks and canons, save that while the monks occupied the wastes, the friars made for the towns. They were even more un-English in provenance than the monks, deriving as they did from Francis of Assisi, Dominic the Spaniard, and groups of hermits from the Levant and the Abruzzi, though it is worth noting that just as the English Stephen Harding had been the steadfast leader at Cîteaux so Haymo of Faversham and another man of Kent, the shadowy but significant Simon Stock, were the effective reorganizers of the Minors and the Carmelites throughout Europe in general. In the first beginnings, however, Agnellus and Albert of Pisa among the Minors, and Jordan of Saxony among the Preachers, were the pillars. Moreover, the friars were more truly international and more thoroughly centralized than the monks and canons. Whereas the latter belonged each to his own abbey, the friar had no permanent tie within his province, and might even be transferred even outside his native land to learn, to teach, to preach or even to govern. His ultimate superior and legislative body was not a large chapter of prelates, but a single Minister or Master-General, who could use his subjects as might seem best for the ends of the order. Finally, the orders of friars had a very different centre of gravity from that of the monks. The mother to whom the latter turned (when they were not altogether autonomous) was the original founding abbey— Cluny or Cîteaux or Prémontré—and in the day of their apogee these abbeys were centres of Christendom almost as influential (though in a different way) as Rome, but the friars were from the first pivoted upon the Roman Curia not, indeed, as firmly and exclusively as has been the case since the sixteenth century, but still really and effectively.

The coming of the friars, besides laying down another grid upon the ecclesiastical map of Europe, drew together the already existing network of academic connections. The pull of Paris had long been supreme. Thither, for almost a century, had gone all the ablest youths of England who hoped to make a career in the Church. Many of them returned, and in the sequel helped to give England two universities on the Parisian model, so that very soon, with interesting but inessential differences, Oxford became another Paris, ultimately rivalling her mother in attraction. So to England came one by one the great waves of theological discipline with their appropriate techniques and text-books—the Victorines, Peter the Lombard, Peter Comestor and the most celebrated commentators on the Sentences or on the Scriptures. This two-way traffic continued throughout the thirteenth century. Grosseteste, Alexander of Hales, Roger Bacon, Robert Kilwardby, John Pecham and Duns Scotus went to Paris and Rome and Cologne, and all save Duns returned sooner or later to this country; to England in return came the disciples of Bonaventure, Albert the Great and Thomas Aquinas; while all the while English masters were writing their commentaries on the Lombard. And it was from Paris that the English Church drew so many of its bishops and chief dignitaries. It would be no exaggeration to say that England drew from the Continent either immediately or at second or third hand, the lore of every decree and of every advance made in the matter and technique of theological and biblical learning. Yet perhaps this is a misleading statement. What should have been said is that English masters and students both gave and received all their learning to and from the common pool of Western Christendom. The Englishmen who have just been mentioned contributed as truly to the total growth of Christian learning in their day as did the Italians or the Germans. We think of Stephen Langton as the principal author of Magna Carta, but he has securer titles to universal fame as the scholar who divided the Bible for us into chapters, and who gave to the Church the *Veni Sancte Spiritus*.

A similar judgment might be made, all proportions guarded, of the other great department of ecclesiastical science, the canon law. Here indeed one country, Italy, and one university, Bologna, had a place apart even more completely than had Paris in theology. Yet there were English masters, both at Bologna and later at Oxford, as well as English students; Oxford used the same books and studied the same questions, and one has only to look at the library catalogues of a medieval abbey or cathedral chapter to see what a space the books of the great decretalists

and theorists of the thirteenth century occupied in the presses
and in the minds of the abbots and bishops' officials of the age.

The last decades of the thirteenth century, where our allotted
period ends, are marked for England by no revolutionary or
catastrophic event, though in the larger field of Europe the pontificate of Boniface VIII might well be regarded as such. Nevertheless, to those who know what came after the signs of change
are apparent. Though the connection with the Continent was as
close as ever, the time had passed when external influences upon
the English Church were welcome and beneficent. England had
long made her own the administrative and disciplinary methods
of the centralized Church, and Rome had ceased to bestow
liberty and law. The high-water mark of the medieval Church
had been reached, and the tide drawing back was draining the
basins it had filled. The papacy, in certain external ways at least,
was beginning to live upon the Church rather than to give it
pasture. At the same time the schools had passed the zenith of
their glory. Philosophy was parting company with theology, and
both were losing touch with the life around them. The secular
state had appeared in France, and even in England the development of a conscious national spirit was apparent. The first
Statute of Provisors, the first seizure of the alien priories, the out-
break for the first time of something like a national war between
England and France, the contest between Edward I and Archbishop Winchelsey, himself the last of the great Parisian masters
to be Archbishop of Canterbury—all these were symptomatic of
their age. Their significance, indeed, must not be exaggerated;
it was on the political, diplomatic level; it did not alter the
peaceful functioning of the body of the Church nor did it trouble
the minds of clerics or lay-folk to any marked degree. It was,
however, the prelude to another act, with which we are not
concerned.

In conclusion, we may cast our eyes back across the two centuries of our review. Within that period connections of every
kind between the Continent and England became closer than
they had ever been in the past and closer than they were destined
ever to be in the future. During those centuries, the learning and
thought of England was indistinguishable from that of the other

countries of Western Europe, or rather, it formed an integral contribution to the common store. In those centuries, also, the Church in England was integrated into, or perhaps we should rather say vitally informed by, the centralized, organized Western Church. What had in previous centuries been a union of faith, love and loyalty became now a union of law, discipline and authority. In those centuries the solidarity of Western Christendom, and of England as a province of the larger unity, became explicit; perhaps it would be more exact to say that it was universally recognized as axiomatic.

3

THE LATER MIDDLE AGES

W. A. Pantin

THE underlying problem to be considered here is this: what amount of give and take, of spiritual imports and exports, was there between England and the Continent during the fourteenth and fifteenth centuries? In earlier periods we know what Augustine or Theodore, Lanfranc or Anselm had to bring to England, and what Boniface or Stephen Harding had to give to the Continent. In this later period, is this process of give and take continued, accelerated, or slowed down? In trying to answer this question, we must bear in mind that there were two forces at work in the English Church from the thirteenth century onwards, one centripetal, the other centrifugal. On the one hand there was a great increase in centralization and mobility, as shown in the ever-growing centralization of the Church, through the exercise of the papal *plenitudo potestatis*; in the greater mobility which was implied in the organization, for instance, both of the friars and (in theory at least) of the universities; in the common west European intellectual heritage, as shown in the common stock of books in current use, so that if we were presented with a medieval library catalogue, it might at first sight be difficult to identify the country of its origin. From all these points of view, the English Church was more than ever part of an international whole. On the other hand there was the growing development of national characteristics in all kinds of ways, negative and positive, noble and ignoble, ranging from a dislike of foreigners to vernacular mysticism—from the grumblings of the Good Parliament to the *Revelations* of Dame Julian, and these forces, at work *mutatis mutandis* in other countries also, tended to divide Christendom. We must not think that 'nationalism' was something invented at the Renaissance or even in the later middle ages, or that medieval men, including Englishmen, saw themselves as all subjects of the Holy Roman Empire. On the contrary, since the eleventh century there had been highly organized 'national' states and deep political and racial divisions and rivalries and antipathies; I doubt if medieval Englishmen would have stood for being ruled by Scottish or Dutch or German kings as their descendants did. The result was that deep and real political divisions coexisted with an international Church and an international culture, and one of the most remarkable and worthwhile achievements of medieval England was precisely to combine genuine catholicity with genuine Englishry.

This survey of the relations between the English Church and the Continent falls into two parts: first the constitutional and quasi-political contacts, with which I shall deal briefly, because the subject is well worn; and secondly the intellectual and religious contacts, with which I shall deal rather more fully, since it is perhaps less familiar ground.

I. *The constitutional and quasi-political relations of the English Church and the Continent.*

Every one was deeply and constantly conscious that the English Church was part of the universal Catholic Church, in communion with and subject to the Holy See. Whatever men felt about the practical effects of this, no one challenged it in principle, except of course the Wycliffites, and that was not an encouraging example; indeed it may be said that it was Wyclif who effectively killed any possibility of an English 'Gallican' theory developing. The centralization of the Church made itself felt in various ways: in legislation, for instance, through a body of universal canon law, taught in the universities and applied in the Church courts; and a curious by-product of this internationalism was the scarcity of English canonist writers, presumably because English canon law students were content with continental books, though it was an English canonist, Thomas Fastolf, who was the author of the earliest known collection of the Decisions of the Roman Court of the Rota. Centralization was also effected in the judicial sphere by appeals to Rome and by the use of papal-judges delegate, and in the sphere of ecclesiastical patronage by papal provisions. How did this work in practice?

During the period of the Avignonese Papacy (1309–78), papal provisions were at their height, but the provision of aliens into English benefices was less than is generally supposed. Bishops came to be appointed normally by papal provision, but, from the time of Edward III onwards, they were generally provided at the king's nomination, and the appointment of aliens to English bishoprics was almost unknown. The ordinary parish clergy were hardly affected by the provision of aliens. It was the cathedral chapters, the deaneries, prebends and archdeaconries, that were most heavily affected by the papal provision of aliens; the benefices held by aliens were few but costly. The practical effects of papal provisions were exaggerated in contemporary opinion, but the system was important in several ways. First, a great opportunity was missed : papal provision might have been used as an instrument of reform, for appointing men who would otherwise not have been available, as when the see of York had been offered to S. Bonaventure in the thirteenth century. Instead, the king and the pope made a tacit bargain; they divided the prebends and dignities between the royal and papal officials, while the king got the bishoprics for his nominees. It was a working system which showed more practical common sense than idealism. Secondly papal provision was important because it provoked so much strong opposition and anti-papal feeling. This was the more so because there was an endemic dislike of foreigners, especially of foreign ecclesiastics, throughout the thirteenth and fourteenth centuries, and this was exacerbated by the Hundred Years War and by the English victories; when God was so obviously on the side of the English, it seemed intolerable that the pope should be so French.

The opposition to aliens and to provisions was led by the lay magnates and the commons in parliament; the latter in 1376 complained of the 'brokers of benefices in the sinful city of Avignon.' King Edward III was perhaps not much interested in this agitation, preferring to get what he wanted from the pope by diplomacy, but he yielded to pressure, and the result was the Statutes of Provisors (1351) and of Praemunire (1353). These were at first rather halfheartedly applied, but they were renewed in 1390 and more strictly enforced. What happened in fact was that while the papal provision of the king's nominees to bishoprics continued, the provision of aliens to English benefices was almost unknown after 1400. Pope Martin V tried hard to compel the unfortunate Archbishop Chichele to have the Statute of Provisors repealed, but as Professor Jacob has said, he was 'knocking at an open door'; English churchmen would have liked to see papal provisions in use, for instance to promote university graduates, but they were powerless to persuade the king and parliament to repeal the statute. The working compromise or checkmate between Church and State, crown and papacy remained, very much to the king's advantage. At the end of the fifteenth and the beginning of the sixteenth century we find a number of Italian bishops in the sees of Worcester, Salisbury and Hereford; this at first sight looks like a shocking piece of papal encroachment, but it is in fact the measure of the royal control over the English Church. These Italians were valuable to the king as envoys between the king and the Roman Curia, and so it was convenient to reward them or pay them with English bishoprics; it was rather like lending an English aerodrome or a London square for the use of the Americans.

I think that after 1400 the causes of Anglo-Roman friction were much reduced; there is an absence of xenophobia in the fifteenth century, in contrast to the fourteenth century. If his contemporaries made objections to Henry Beaufort's getting a cardinal's hat or a papal legateship, it was because they disliked Beaufort, not because they disliked the pope.

How did the Great Schism in the Papacy in 1378 and the Conciliar Movement that followed affect the English Church, and what part did the English play in those events? The first thing to notice is that in the Schism the fissure ran along national lines, illustrating that centrifugal force to which I have already referred. Pope Urban VI at Rome was supported by Englishmen, Germans and Italians; Pope Clement VII at Avignon was supported by Frenchmen and Scots. At first this meant some enthusiasm among the English for the Roman pope, *Urbanus noster,* as against the anti-pope supported by the wicked, schis-

matic Frenchmen and Scots; but of course, in the long run, the
Schism caused great scandal. Attempts were therefore made to
find a means of ending the Schism, especially between 1390 and
1417, in which leading parts were played by the universities of
Oxford and Paris and by the kings of England, France and
Germany. As a means of ending the Schism, the English favoured
the holding of a General Council, rather than the enforced
resignation or repudiation of the popes, which was the way
favoured by the university of Paris; the English were perhaps
unwilling to admit that their pope could be the wrong pope.

At the Council of Constance (1414–18), the English delegation, especially Bishop Hallum of Salisbury, and behind them,
the English king, Henry V, played an active and very creditable
part in restoring unity and the recognition of a single pope; this
was one of England's greatest contributions to European history.
At Constance and at the later Councils, such as Basel, there was
a three-part programme : unity, orthodoxy and reform of head
and members of the Church. The English were enthusiastic for
the cause of unity (as we have seen) and for orthodoxy, which
meant the condemnation of Wyclif and Hus and the Hussites;
they felt the more strongly on this, since they had recently themselves had their first experience of heresy. As to the cause of
reform, it would not be fair to say the English were lukewarm or
isolationist, but they envisaged reform 'with a difference.' The
English did not share the anti-papalism of the conciliar die-
hards; their attitude towards the papacy was loyal, if critical, in
the tradition of Grosseteste, in fact. Above all their ideas of
reform were essentially practical, as we can see from looking at
such documents as the petitions for reform submitted by Richard
Ullerston in 1408 for presentation to the General Council; or the
similar articles presented by the university of Oxford in 1414;
or the Concordat between England and Pope Martin V in 1418.
In all these the greatest stress is laid on practical points, such as
that the pope should choose cardinals from all nations and with
the consent of the existing cardinals; that abuse of dispensations,
pluralities, or excessive fees should be avoided ; and above all that
recent appropriations of churches by monasteries should be
revoked or restricted, while the exemption of monasteries from

the jurisdiction of the bishops is attacked. Here we have something of that preoccupation with pastoral efficiency and discipline which we find in Thomas Gascoigne, the Oxford theologian of a generation or two later, and there is also a resemblance to the views of an earlier figure, Bishop Grosseteste whom these reformers are fond of quoting—but without Grosseteste's love of theorizing; we do not hear now of the sun-pope giving light to the moon- and star-bishops.

English churchmen and English statesmen had found a reasonable working compromise in the relations between Church and State and between England and the Papacy; no doubt this was capable of improvement, but men were unwilling to theorize about it. A very striking thing about the English Church in this period is the almost complete absence, so far as one can see, of anything like a Gallican doctrine—of that theorizing about the relation of the pope to the Church, to the Councils, and to the ancient canon law, as set forth in France in the Council of 1406 and the ordinances of 1407, and in the writings of theologians like Gerson. In France, to the Gallicans, the 'liberties of the Gallican Church' were something that you defended against the pope; in England, the 'liberties of the English Church' were something that you defended against the Crown, by keeping the Crown to the observance of Article 1 of Magna Carta, by continuing to present grievances against lay encroachments in the *articuli cleri*, and so forth. What Englishmen were at pains to defend against the papacy was not the liberties of the English Church, but the liberties and rights of the English Crown, and the rights of patrons from the king downwards as guaranteed by English secular law. This defence was left to lay action, notably in the Statutes of Provisors and Praemunire; the English prelates felt constrained to make formal protests against these statutes, and in 1428 Archbishop Chichele went in tears to Parliament to try to persuade it to repeal the statutes. English churchmen had their own feelings about how papal provisions worked, feelings sometimes expressed very explosively by chroniclers; but they did not formulate a doctrinal theory about such matters, so far as we know, though there may be treatises lurking in manuscripts yet to be discovered. The nearest approach to an expression of a

Gallican theory seems to have been in that episode of 1428 already referred to, when Martin V was pressing Chichele to procure the repeal of the repeal of the Statute of Provisors and proceeded to suspend Chichele from his legatine functions. Chichele, hearing that a bull of suspension was on its way, made in advance a formal legal appeal from the pope to a future General Council. So much is clear from contemporary documents, but Thomas Gascoigne, writing some years later, goes further and says that the pope also excommunicated the English bishops (which is difficult to believe), and that the English bishops appealed to a General Council, because, they said, a General Council was superior to the pope, whereas, Gascoigne comments, they had often previously said that the pope was above a General Council; Gascoigne liked to have a dig at bishops. This appeal from the pope to a General Council here seems to be a legal manœuvre rather than a theological argument on Gallican lines. On the whole therefore it seems that a Gallican theory was conspicuously absent in England. Why was this so? This was perhaps due, first, to a native English practical caution, such as we shall also see reflected in English attitudes to mystical currents; and Englishmen had established their *modus vivendi*, to the great advantage of the English Crown. Perhaps something was also due to the traditional English devotion to the Holy See, going back to Anglo-Saxon times, to the memory of 'our father Gregory, who gave us baptism.' Above all, there was probably at work a revulsion from Wycliffism; Wyclif was the anti-papal writer Englishmen best knew.

II. *The intellectual and religious contacts of the English Church and the Continent.*

The first question we may ask is, what use was made of institutional channels such as the universities, the friars, and the Roman Curia? The universities were supposed to be *studia generalia*, open to all the world; how far were they really international in the later middle ages? Were they thronged with the ecclesiastical equivalent of Rhodes Scholars? Here we may compare the coming and going of scholars like John of Salisbury and Peter of Blois in the twelfth century, or the flocking of scholars like S. Edmund or Pecham to Paris in the thirteenth century. On the one hand, how far did English scholars go to foreign universities in the later middle ages? We may take a cross-section from the history of Christ Church, Canterbury. About the year 1300 we find the Prior of Canterbury, the great Henry of Eastry, not only maintaining monk students at Paris, but also sending secular students, promising boys from Kent, to study at Oxford, Paris, Orleans and Bologna. Probably many English students went to Paris in the first third of the fourteenth century. For instance, Walter Burley studied at Oxford, Paris and Toulouse; he dedicated his commentary on Aristotle's *Politics* to Pope Clement VI because he had admired Clement's lectures at Paris. But by the middle of the century the stream had probably dried up, first on account of the Hundred Years' War and then on account of the Great Schism; and perhaps the intellectual rivalry between Paris and Oxford, of which Richard de Bury speaks, may also have hindered intercourse. In contrast Scottish students continued to flock to Paris, and there were long periods when the 'English Nation' at Paris consisted (*horribile dictu*) of Scots and Germans! To return to the evidence of Christ Church, Canterbury, we find monks going to Italy in the late fourteenth and fifteenth centuries; Thomas Chillenden, the building prior, studied canon law at the Roman Curia, and above all, William Sellyng, one of the leading English humanists, studied in Italy. A considerable number of English students can be traced at Italian universities in the fifteenth century. A new trend can be observed in the early sixteenth century, when we find some Canterbury monks at Louvain. Probably the general pattern of student migration was first to Paris, in the early fourteenth century, then after a break, to Italy in the fifteenth century; but this is a subject which needs more research.

A converse question may be asked : to what extent did foreign students come to England? Probably not many seculars, but a few distinguished individuals can be traced, such as Giovanni Contarini, a noble Venetian, later Patriarch of Constantinople, who studied at Oxford *c.* 1392-9. More important was the number of foreign friars who came to Oxford and Cambridge, both of which constituted *studia generalia* in the scholastic organization of the orders. Of the friars traceable at Oxford, a notable percentage were foreigners: 10 per cent among the Dominicans, 5 per cent among the Franciscans, and as much as 17 per cent among the Austin Friars. Among the foreign Franciscan students was Peter of Candia, a Greek, born c. 1340 in Crete, who became a Franciscan, studied at Norwich, Oxford and Paris, and became pope as Alexander V in 1408—the only pope in history to have been a student of Oxford. The Austin Friars in particular made a policy of sending foreign friars to Oxford, Cambridge and Paris about 1355; and this was the more remarkable, since Oxford and Cambridge were homes of the nominalist teaching of which the rulers of the Austin Friars disapproved.

Besides the universities and the friars, the Roman Curia, especially when it was at Avignon, was important as a meeting-place for men and a clearing house for ideas, as well as for ecclesiastical business. Visits to the Curia might have a crucial effect on a man's intellectual career; thus it was at the Curia that Richard Fitz-Ralph was commissioned to write his great *Summa* to explain the Catholic faith to the Armenians, and it was there that his meeting with the Archbishop of Trau encouraged him in his work against the friars. It was at the Curia that Adam Easton, monk and later cardinal, spent years studying the Old Testament and learning Hebrew, wrote his *magnum opus* against Marsilius, John of Jandun and Wyclif (dedicating his book to Urban VI as 'monarch of the world'), and became the enthusiastic advocate of S. Brigit of Sweden.

Next we may consider the interchange between England and the Continent as reflected in personalities and schools of thought. Among the scholastic theologians and philosophers of the period, some Englishmen were very influential, often in a controversial and disruptive manner. Thus William of Occam, as a political thinker and still more as a philosopher, was perhaps the one English thinker who had the greatest influence throughout Europe between 1300 and 1500, or indeed until the time of Bacon or Newton; he acted as the great solvent of the classic scholasticism of the thirteenth century. Richard Fitz-Ralph was another international figure, who spent much time at the Roman Curia; he was very important, especially in the development of

English thought, as in his effect on Wyclif, but I do not know whether his work had as much currency abroad as one might expect, apart from his *Summa* for the Armenians. John Wyclif was most remarkable in this context. While he was a peculiarly English and even insular figure, in comparison with Occam or Fitz-Ralph, yet in the long run he had a much greater influence abroad than at home. As a really influential intellectual movement Wycliffism did not long survive its founder in England; but transplanted by his followers to Bohemia, taken up by Hus and the Hussites, it became an enormous force, both intellectually and politically. It is significant that the most important manuscripts of Wyclif's works are to be found in the libraries of Eastern Europe.

In another intellectual field, there were English schoolmen who had great influence abroad, namely the interesting group of scientists—logicians, mathematicians, physicists—at work at Oxford and especially at Merton in the early fourteenth century, such men as Walter Burley, John Dumbleton, Richard Swyneshead (known as the *Calculator*) and William Heytesbury; manuscripts of their works are to be found all over the Continent, and they form an important link between medieval and renaissance science.

What of converse influences : how far was the work of foreign schoolmen current in England? There was certainly one bestseller of foreign origin in the early fourteenth century : Giles of Rome, whose work *De regimine principum* was the standard text-book of political theory, to be found in every respectable English library. But works like Dante's *De monarchia* or the writings of Marsilius of Padua or John of Jandun were I think hardly known in medieval England; I do not think that Wyclif had any knowledge of them, though they would have been very much to his purpose. It was only an Englishman who lived at the Curia, like Adam Easton, who knew about them. Another curious example of insularity—or was it insulation?—is the fact that the very fine library of Austin Friars at York in the late fourteenth century had no copies of the great Italian writers of that order who wrote in defence of papal power, men like James of Viterbo, Augustinus Triumphus, Alexander de S. Elpidio.

There is another line of intellectual development in which English writers of this period had something to give to the Continent; this was in the very beginnings of humanism, in that enthusiastic interest in classical studies, as then available, in ancient history, ancient philosophers, ancient writers, in which English scholars excelled. This interest, in its early stages, can hardly be called humanism, but it might be labled pre-humanism or classicism. It goes back to the *Policraticus* of John of Salisbury in the twelfth century, was revived by the Franciscan, John of Wales, in the late thirteenth century, and was carried on in the fourteenth century by the Dominicans Nicholas Trivet, Robert Holcot, and Thomas Waleys, and by the secular Richard de Bury. Thus we find Trivet at Avignon being asked by an Italian cardinal and a French pope to write commentaries on Seneca's plays and Livy's history (*c.* 1314–19); this was the first time since the twelfth century that any one had written a commentary on a classical, literary or historical text. At this time there was easier access to classical texts north of the Alps than south of them, and it was a very important step forwards to the Renaissance, when Italian scholars came north, as when Petrarch came to the Curia at Avignon; they found classical manuscripts in northern libraries (as Petrarch did in the Sorbonne library) and met northern scholars already interested in the classics. In this fruitful intercommunication or cross-fertilization between Italian and northern scholarship, Englishmen took a not unimportant part; we have seen that it was an Italian cardinal who asked Trivet to comment on Seneca. Very soon of course it was the Italian humanists who shot forward, and by the fifteenth century it was Englishmen like William Sellyng who made literary pilgrimages to Italy. The Italian humanists came to despise the northern scholars who had once helped them—'enfants drus et bien nourris qui battent leur nourrice, le Moyen âge,' as Henri Bremond once wrote of the Renaissance humanists.

It may be asked what has all this, the part played by Englishmen in the rise of humanism, to do with the English Church and religion in England? The answer is that it has a good deal of relevance. In the first place, one of the subjects that most fascinated these early English pre-humanists was the virtues and the teaching of the 'good pagans' of antiquity, particularly the Greek philosophers. John of Wales, for instance, wrote whole treatises about the moral virtues as exemplified in Plato, Socrates and Aristotle. Now this touches closely on an age-long controversy among Christian theologians, namely the problem of pagan morality; is our fallen human nature totally depraved, or is it only wounded and robbed, like the man who fell among thieves : *vulneratus in naturalibus, spoliatus gratuitis*? Secondly the renewed interest in classical writers also brought with it that attention to early Christian writers and fathers, and especially to S. Jerome, which was to be such a feature of the Christian renaissance; we can see this process already at work in the fifteenth century in Thomas Gascoigne and later in John Colet. Thirdly the long established friendliness of English churchmen towards humanism and humanists helps to explain, later, the welcome given for instance by Warham, Fisher and More to Erasmus, and more particularly the attitude of More, combining an enthusiasm for humanism with a heroic attachment to tradition—an attitude which some have found puzzling. It was a notable feature of early English humanism, especially in the fifteenth century, that whereas in Italy, from an early stage, there was often conflict and hostility between humanists and traditional schoolmen, in England there was no such conflict, at least until well after 1500. Rather there was a determination to make the best of both worlds, the old learning and the new, as is reflected in the contemporary library catalogues, and is symbolized rather pleasantly in one of the books in the library of Canterbury College, Oxford, which contained a papal bull for the Jubilee of S. Thomas of Canterbury (1470) bound up in one volume with an early printed edition of Plutarch on the education of children.

There remains a further question : how much contact was there between England and the Continent in more purely religious movements, including the monastic life? There was of course nothing comparable with the Anglo-Norman monastic plantation or the coming of the Cistercians and the Friars. But there were some new monastic movements, of continental origin, small in numbers, but important in their impact on England. First there were the Bridgettines, an order of men and women, founded by the Swedish mystic S. Brigit, who had early attracted the interest and admiration of some Englishmen like Adam Easton; this order was introduced into England in 1415, by King Henry V, when he founded the monastery which later settled at Syon in Middlesex. Secondly there were the Friars Observant, a reformed branch of the Franciscans, also introduced into England under royal patronage, this time by Edward IV in 1481. Finally there were the Carthusians; these were not of course a new importation, since they had been here since the twelfth century, but they were a new growth; between 1340 and 1414 the number of England charterhouses rose from two to nine. The popularity of the charterhouses, and especially of those on the outskirts of the great towns, as at London, Coventry and Hull, is very much in line with contemporary continental practice, where we find charterhouses established outside towns like Bruges, Cologne, Trier, Mainz, Dijon. These three orders were important; they enjoyed royal patronage and became recognized as the strictest, most spiritual orders in an age of low-pressure observance, and they were destined to make heroic resistance to suppression in the sixteenth century.

Of a more personal character is the contact between English and Italian mysticism in the person of William Flete, the English Austin Friar and Cambridge graduate, who went out to settle as a hermit near Siena, and became the friend and disciple of S. Catherine of Siena; his letters to his English brethren survive. I do not know of any like personal contacts with the German or Flemish mystics.

The outstanding achievement of fourteenth century England was of course the school of English mystics, Rolle, Hilton, the author of the *Cloud of Unknowing*, and Julian of Norwich, and here one asks, what had they to give to or to receive from the continental mystics? Here there is need for more study, but it looks as though, apart from the currency of Rolle's less sensational works in Latin form on the Continent, there was less connection with contemporary continental currents than one might expect. At least one English mystic, the author of the *Cloud*, owed much to the influence of the pseudo-Denys, via a continental commentator, Thomas Gallus of Vercelli, but that can hardly be regarded as a contemporary Continental contact. This comparative insularity is in interesting contrast to the eleventh and twelfth centuries, when the writings of men like John of Fécamp, Anselm, and Eadmer had international currency, and easily become confused with each other, or when Gilbert of Hoyland takes up where S. Bernard leaves off, in the sermons on the Canticles. Perhaps it was that the rise in various countries of vernacular mysticism and piety, and connected with this, the rise of the devout and educated layman, though in themselves among the most exciting and magnificent phenomena of the late medieval Church, nevertheless tended to separate European piety into self-contained compartments. At any rate it meant that every one was dependent on the selective enterprise of translators.

On the other hand, on a less mystical, more workaday level, the printing press came to give easy currency in English libraries (to judge from the contemporary catalogues) to many kinds of continental books, not only standard works like Ludolph of Saxony's *Life of Christ, John Nyder on the Ten Commandments,* or *Henry of Hesse,* but also more out of the way works, which might not otherwise have reached English libraries, like the sermons of Nicholas Blony of Posen, or the 'Rosary of preachable sermons' of Bernardino de Busti. One wonders whether this transportation of sermons all over Europe ever produced comic results, like the modern stories of English rustics being treated to sermons intended for the Indian Army.

There are some examples where we can try to trace and test religious influences from the Continent. Margery Kempe, of King's Lynn, in the early fifteenth century, is an interesting example of a not uncommon type, the devout laywoman, even if she was rather an abnormal, hysterical specimen. Among other things she reminds us of one means of Anglo-continental contact, namely pilgrimages; Margery was an inveterate pilgrim, visiting Rome, Jerusalem, Compostella—a kind of spiritualized wife of Bath. Of course people can travel all over the world without becoming cosmopolitan—*caelum non animum mutant—* and Margery's foreign conversation was limited to such phrases as 'Bone christian, pray pur me.' But contact with so many other devout people, lay and clerical, all over the Mediterranean world must have impressed her. At Rome she got an introduction to the former maidservant of S. Brigit of Sweden (one of Margery's heroines), who told her, through an interpreter, that S. Brigit was 'goodly and meek to every creature, and had a laughing cheer' ; and she heard a German priest preach about S. Brigit, when she visited the saint's house. We know the books she had read to her (she was herself illiterate) : some English, Hilton and Rolle ; some continental, the *Meditations on the Life of Christ,* wrongly attributed to S. Bonaventure, the *Stimulus amoris* of James of Milan, S. Brigit ; and we may compare these with the books read to another pious laywoman later in the fifteenth century, the Lady Cicely, mother of King Edward IV ; Hilton, the pseudo-Bonaventure, the *Golden Legend* of Jacobus de Voragine, S. Mechtild, S. Catherine of Siena, S. Brigit of Sweden. Margery Kempe's autobiography quotes such continental women mystics as Mary of Oignies and Elizabeth of Hungary. It should be remembered that the later middle ages was a great period of women mystics ; Miss Hope Emily Allen, in her edition of Margery Kempe, lists four Italian, three northern French, two Swedish and about ten German examples, such as S. Mechtild of Magdeburg, S. Mechtild of Hakeborn, S. Gertrude, Blessed Dorothea of Prussia. These no doubt in some way formed models for Margery Kempe ; not that she is likely to have had direct knowledge of them, but as Miss Allen suggests, her spiritual directors probably knew about them, and this helps to explain why they were so sympathetic to her in spite of her eccentricities ; it helped them to 'place' Margery as an abnormal specimen of a well recognized type. Late medieval piety and mysticism had characteristic dangers as well as characteristic virtues : excessive emotionalism ; occasional heterodoxy (such as a tendency to pantheism) ; or antinomialism (placing oneself above ordinary morality) ; the French theologian, Gerson, had drawn attention to these dangers. Margery Kempe adopted the emotionalism of the age in an extreme form, but to her credit she avoided heresy and antinomianism, and was indeed strongly moralistic. On the very spot where this lecture was delivered, in the hall of Lambeth Palace, Margery rebuked the Archbishop's servants for swearing great oaths, and the Archbishop himself for allowing them to do so. With all her eccentricities, she had a strong dose of robust Christian good sense.

Another example where continental influences can be seen at work, this time carefully strained and checked, is in the book called *The Chastising of God's Children* (recently edited by Mr. E. Colledge). This is a Middle English mystical treatise written about 1382 or soon after. It draws very largely on continental mystical sources, especially Ruysbroek; Suso's *Horologium Divinae Sapientiae,* and an Italian treatise, the *Epistola Solitarii* (on S. Brigit); but it is very selective in the use of these writers, and the author is concerned to repress excessive 'enthusiasm,' emotionalism, seeking of sign and wonders; he stresses the importance of recognizing and repressing heresy, and presses the claims of liturgical worship as against private devotions. All this I think shows a rather characteristic English caution and common sense; one is reminded of Margery Kempe's travelling companions; when Margery exclaimed at the dinner table: 'It is full merry in Heaven,' they used to reply: 'Why speak ye so much of the mirth that is in Heaven? Ye know it not and ye have not been there, no more than we have.' So I think that while continental influences were at work, they were to some extent filtered through English caution.

One of the outstanding features of religious life in medieval England, as elsewhere in Europe, was a growing concentration of devotion on the Person of Christ, through 'affective' meditation on the mysteries of the life and especially the passion of Christ, devotion to the Holy Name, and so forth; and this is reflected not only in the religious literature of the period, but also in the art and religious drama. How far was this development, in England, a native growth, how much was due to continental influences? The history of Christo-centric piety in medieval England needs to be written. All that one can say at present is that this development has a long native history; we can already see it well developed in the writings of Ailred of Rievaulx, especially in his instructions to his recluse sister on the method of meditation; and the famous hymn, *Jesu dulcis memoria,* was probably an English Cistercian composition of the late twelfth century. In

the thirteenth century this devotion was reinforced by some continental writings, particularly those of the Franciscan school,
such as the *Arbor Crucifixi* of S. Bonaventure, and the meditations
on the life of Christ attributed to him; and in the fourteenth
century it finds native expression in Rolle and Dame Julian. In
fact the native and continental strands are difficult to dis-
entangle. A particularly interesting example is the devotion to the
Holy Name of Jesus. This was very much fostered on the
Continent by S. Bernardino of Siena (1380–1444), and the
fifteenth century Oxford theologian, Thomas Gascoigne, speaks
of him and his disciple S. John Capistrano with approval; and
Gascoigne had a characteristic habit of writing the sacred mono-
gram I H C in the margins of his books. The unwary student
might suppose that this devotion was introduced into England
from that Italian source, but in fact we find it well developed in
the previous century by Richard Rolle, for instance. Thus we
have here two devotional movements, no doubt ultimately
derived from a common source, but working independently, and
then converging.

Finally, what Anglo-continental contacts can be traced in the
ecclesiastical arts? In ecclesiastical architecture, this is on the
whole a period of real insularity. It is true that the English
'Court' style of the early fourteenth century, out of which the
Perpendicular style developed, owed something to French influences; but the Perpendicular style, once it had fully developed
in the course of the fourteenth century, came to be a peculiarly
English style. Whereas Durham might have been built in
Normandy, or Westminster Abbey in the Ile de France, the nave
of Canterbury, or King's College Chapel, Cambridge, could only
have been built in England. In music, on the other hand, there
was much more coming and going. In the *Ars nova*, the poly-
phony of the fourteenth and fifteenth centuries, French musicians
first excelled, such as Guillaume de Machaut in the fourteenth
century; then English composers and singers come to the fore in
the early fifteenth century, of whom the greatest is John
Dunstable (d. 1453); and the English in turn influenced the
Burgundian school of the later fifteenth century, like Guillaume
Dufay (d. 1474). This was a period when royal and noble patron-

age counted for much in music, more than was pleasing to some ecclesiastical reformers; already in 1408 Richard Ullerston was complaining that English lords, ecclesiastical and secular, set too much store on building up private choirs of singers for their chapels, so that all the benefices they can collect will not suffice for this purpose.

4

THE SIXTEENTH CENTURY

Professor Owen Chadwick

AMONG the manuscripts of Corpus Christi College, Oxford, is a list of the books which an Oxford bookseller, John Dorne, sold to his customers during the year 1520. It is a fascinating list because it enables us to see what the dons and the undergraduates of 1520 were buying, and how much they were paying for each book. They were buying a lot of novels; a fair number of grammars and text-books for their examinations; a surprising number of almanacs; texts of the classics; liturgical books; volumes of sermons; works of the fathers; one or two medical texts-books; Dorne was frequently selling copies of various works by Erasmus. Towards the end of February 1520 someone came into the shop and bought Luther's *De Potestate Papae*. So far as I know that is the earliest actual evidence for the buying of Luther's books in England, though there is little doubt that the Austin Friars in the house of their order at Cambridge, on the site of what is now the Cavendish Laboratory, were reading Luther's books earlier than that, for Luther was one of the leading theologians of their order. Friars of that house like Robert Barnes and Miles Coverdale would have been naturally and rapidly put in touch with the writings of their colleague in Germany. During the summer Dorne shut up his shop and went off to the Continent to fetch more books from the printing presses of the Rhineland. He opened his shop again on 5 August. Henceforth works of Luther began quietly to sell : the commentary on Galatians; a copy of the Leipzig disputation; and several copies of *De Potestate Papae*.

The history of the Reformation in England is to a large extent a history of continental influence upon English minds. If you regard the Reformation as beginning with the nailing of the 95

Theses by Luther in 1517, then for the first seventy-five years there is not a single English theologian whom we should naturally regard as an original and constructive thinker. During the whole of what might be called the formative period of reformed theology there is not something which one might call an English school of theology, but only English theologians influenced by Wittenberg, or Zurich, or Geneva, or Strasbourg. With the possible exception of Robert Browne, who does not stand in the main stream of English thought, Hooker is the first person of the Reformation epoch whom Englishmen can claim as an original and constructive thinker—though this is not at all the same thing as supposing that he was uninfluenced by continental thought, for he was profoundly influenced by it. The interest therefore in the study of the relations between the English Church and the continental Churches during the sixteenth century lies in seeing how and why English minds absorbed Continental thought, and why, although they absorbed it, the results were not quite parallel to the results on the Continent. The interest lies in seeing why, though so many Englishmen derived their thought from Luther or Calvin or Zwingli, English theology from Hooker onwards was not precisely Lutheran, nor Calvinist, nor Zwinglian.

Turn to the end of the century—to April 1595 and the pulpit of the university church at Cambridge. A young Fellow of Caius College, by name William Barrett, delivered a sermon in which he attacked the doctrine of predestination to death, and mentioned with a bitter disapprobation the greatest of the continental divines, Calvin, Beza, Zanchius, Peter Martyr, Junius and others. To the distress of many among his audience he talked of *Satanismus Calvini*. On 10 May Barrett was compelled by the heads of several colleges to read a recantation from that same pulpit whence he had delivered his sermon : but he read his recantation in such an irreverent manner that the performance was judged unsatisfactory, and the ensuing controversy split the university. It is not the only sign of that reaction against the continental dominance of English thought. An undergraduate of Caius College asked his tutor to buy for him a copy of Calvin's *Catechism* or Beza's *Confession of Faith,* and was surprised at his tutor's indignation. By 1595 the defence of episcopacy had

already passed from the modest doctrine that bishops were
regrettable but tolerable, through the middling doctrine that
bishops were useful, to the affirmation that bishops were right,
right by historical constitution if not right by apostolic edict.
Hooker had already published his apology for the human reason,
the groundwork *Of the Laws of Ecclesiastical Polity.* Many English churchmen were moving into a phase of antagonism to
Calvinist thought and the presbyterian polity which accompanied
it. This opinion of extreme predestinarianism, said Samuel
Harsnett in a sermon preached at Paul's Cross (a sermon for
which he was censured and silenced by Archbishop Whitgift),

> 'is grown huge and monstrous (like a Goliath), and men do
> shake and tremble at it; yet never a man reacheth to cast
> it down. In the name of the Lord of Hosts we will encounter
> it . . .'

Between the first incoming of Lutheran books in 1518–20, and
the beginnings of the reaction against Calvinism eighty or more
years later, is an epoch in the history of the English Church when
her leaders were in continuous and friendly communication with
the divines of the continental Churches.

The means of communication were those of any other age.
There were books: Englishmen wanted to keep abreast of the
best theological thought from overseas. In the early days, when
bookselling was dangerous, continental printers were glad to sell
books in a market where some were buying in order to read, and
others buying in order to confiscate or burn. It is an interesting
exercise to make a list of the known examples of books written
by the chief divines of Zurich, Zwingli, Bullinger and Gualter,
and either imported into, or printed in, England between 1535
and 1575. There is a trickle in the fifteen-thirties: a wave during
the reign of King Edward VI: and a flood from the accession of
Queen Elizabeth onwards. Even in Henry VIII's reign a corres-
pondent told Bullinger that 'by the sale of your writings alone
you see the booksellers become almost as rich as Croesus': and
in the last half of the century *Bullinger's Decades* became sermons
which Elizabethan clergymen were so encouraged to read from
the pulpit that at one time they almost attained the status of the
English Homilies. Among other books, one thinks above all of

the great translations of the Bible, beginning with Tyndale's and culminating in the Genevan Bible of 1560. This is the Bible known as the Breeches Bible because it rendered Genesis 3 : 7 as 'they sewed fig leaves together, and made themselves breeches.' In was mainly translated by Whittingham and Sampson, and was probably the most scholarly of the English Bibles before the Authorized Version. It captured the English reader not only on its scholarly merits, but because of its utility in comparison with all previous editions. It was the first English Bible to include verse numbers : and soon an edition suitable for the ordinary reader made it the first Bible which was not primarily a lectern Bible. With its occasional Calvinist annotations and Puritan-sounding headings—the story of the daughter of Herodias and the execution of John the Baptist is entitled 'The inconvenience of dancing'—its excellence and its useful size ensured its success. Ninety editions of the whole Bible or of the New Testament were issued during the reign of Elizabeth—and only forty editions of all other versions. Even after the publication of the Authorized Version in 1611 many who were not Puritans continued to use and quote the Genevan version. It was certainly the most influential book imported during the sixteenth century : and it is the supreme representative of the best influences of Puritanism in England. It is too easy for a non-Calvinistic world to see Elizabethan Puritanism only in terms of the Calvinistic underworld, the whitewashing of church walls, the bitterness of the Marprelate Tracts, the strife of collegiate life at the universities, the eccentricities of the preacher wearing three hats in the pulpit or of Fulke with his turkey-gown and 'birding' expeditions; and it is too easy to forget the moral earnestness and reforming power, the doctrinal influence and the impetus to faith exerted by the best English disciples of Calvin. Whether by acceptance or reaction, Calvinism conditioned the history of the Elizabethan Church. Of that influence at its most religious and most scholarly, we may take the Genevan Bible as a symbol.

Then there were letters—it is symbolic that one of the chief sources for English history during that century reposes in the archives of the city of Zurich. There were merchants, theologically minded travellers through the Rhineland and Holy

E

Roman Empire, merchants like Richard Hilles, whose letters turn as readily to the methods of brewing beer as the progress of the Protestant faith.

There were scholars—Englishmen travelling for the sake of study at the continental universities, continentals travelling for the same purpose to Oxford or Cambridge. And the scholar easily shaded off, in those intolerant days, into the refugee. The English scholars who 'clarified' their ideas by enforced exile during the century, from Tyndale and Coverdale and Hooper near the beginning to Puritan leaders like Thomas Cartwright, Francis Johnson and John Smyth, or recusant leaders like Persons and Allen, near the end, make a notable and considerable catalogue. It was inevitable that the longest list of refugees should be found during the reign of Queen Mary, when it was unsafe to stay and yet the government preferred them to go rather than be burnt. Several of the most eminent Elizabethan bishops or archbishops had learnt the pattern of the best reformed churches during their compulsory exile under Queen Mary, usually at Frankfurt or at Zurich—Jewel, Sandys, Grindal, Coxe, Pilkington, Aylmer, Horne and others. For three years, from 1577 to 1580, both the Archbishops of Canterbury and York, as well as the Bishops of London and Winchester, were men who had received their effective training in Protestantism during the Marian exile. Not surprisingly, they were years of lamentable friction between Lambeth and the Queen's government, which did not readily suppose the pattern of Frankfurt or Zurich to be a suitable model for the Church in England. This was one of the reasons why Queen Elizabeth's government could not maintain the comparatively conservative and moderate regulations in liturgy and practice which had been decreed by the so-called Elizabethan Settlement. The government could not do without the leading English divines of the day, and many of those divines had imbibed the air of ecumenical Reformed Protestantism upon the Continent.

Nor were the refugees all from England to the Continent. In the political see-saw, England under Edward VI and Elizabeth gave sanctuary to Protestants fleeing from Charles V, or from the Italian Inquisition, or from the French wars of religion. As late as 1598 the Lady Margaret's Professor of Divinity in the University of Cambridge was a French Huguenot, and he had been preceded by a line of distinguished foreigners who held chairs or lectureships in the universities. In the reign of Edward VI the Regius professorships of divinity at Oxford and Cambridge were both refugees from the Continent : and because these two divines were two of the most distinguished thinkers in Europe, their presence affected momentously the history of the Church of England.

The Italian Peter Martyr Vermigli, who went to the chair at Oxford, was the first don to keep a wife in college. That wife, whom her friends remembered as a godly and delightful woman, died in Oxford—but the reign of Mary came and her bones suffered ill-treatment—and so at the accession of Elizabeth she was reburied of set purpose in the tomb of S. Frideswide, in the cathedral, that there might be no more desecration ; and there they still rest together, the medieval abbess and the godly wife of a Protestant Reformer. Martyr himself could not speak English ; but his *Commonplaces,* whether in the Latin language or in English translation, influenced a generation of English theologians.

The German Martin Bucer, who went to the chair at Cambridge, was the reformer of Strasbourg, a man who had spent his life hammering out a theology to mediate between the poles of Wittenberg and Zurich, one of the two or three chief divines of Protestant Europe. At Cambridge he died in 1551, revered and beloved. Under Queen Mary his body was disinterred from Great S. Mary's and burnt with several of his books in the market square, the Vice-Chancellor and Master of Peterhouse, Dr. Andrew Pern, presiding at part of the ceremony. There are two entries in the Great S. Mary's accounts relating to the purchase of incense to purge the church of its heresy and to remove the interdict placed upon it because Bucer had preached there. At the accession of Elizabeth solemn ceremonies restored him to his honours, the Vice-Chancellor and Master of Peterhouse, Dr. Andrew Pern, again presiding at part of the ceremony.

But before he died he had contributed momentously to the history of the English liturgy. Some scholars assert that Bucer was

more influential than any other single person with the exception
of Cranmer, in the early development of liturgy in the English
language. Whether this is so or not, there are many actions or
phrases still used in English services which owe something to
Bucer—the revival of the particular and ancient mode of cross-
ing the hands to receive the holy sacrament : the questions still
asked of bishops, priests, and deacons before ordination or consecration : the use of the comfortable words in the liturgy : the
declaration that bridegroom and bride are husband and wife—
here a little sentence, there a ritual action, more commonly the
omission of a traditional action. The Anglican services of Ordination and Confirmation owe a main part of their present shape
and structure to Martin Bucer : and if you will consider how
much the religion of the English layman has owed to the due
administration of the sacrament of Confirmation after catechetical preparation, and how Bucer was one of the first to
associate Confirmation with catechetical preparation, you will
perceive the momentous contribution of this distinguished exile
to English religious life.

One other time of Swiss influence needs to be noticed, and the
more because it is only during the last few years that we have
realized its full importance—the contribution of the divines of
Zurich to resisting the challenge of Calvinism during the Elizabethan age.

Zurich and Geneva were far from Wittenberg and the
Lutherans, but they were not in exact agreement. In spite of a
treaty of reconciliation in 1549 (a treaty welcomed in England,
as one of the S. Paul's Cathedral manuscripts hints), they continued to argue over the theology of the Eucharist. Bullinger and
Gualter had seen the reformation at Zurich carried out by the
civil authorities, the city council : Calvin and Beza were determined that at Geneva the spiritual authorities should be independent of the secular authorities, and in their own sphere supreme.
Calvin was afraid of the civil ruler interfering in Church affairs :
Bullinger was afraid of Church authorities prying where they
had no concern and seeking a civil authority to which they had
no right. This discrepancy issued in different attitudes to the
deeds of the Queen of England in her capacity as Supreme

Governor of the Church. If the clergy of the Church of England were ordered to wear a surplice, the Calvinists believed that on conscientious grounds they should refuse, as Miles Coverdale wore a black gown when officiating as a bishop at the consecration of the Archbishop of Canterbury; for the Church must order all things in accordance with scripture, and in doing so should follow the pattern of the best reformed Churches. Bullinger and Gualter agreed that the Church of England should follow the pattern of the best reformed Churches. They agreed in disliking the use of the surplice and the other practices to which the Calvinists objected. But they were ready to recognize that there was an area of adiaphora where the government of a Church had the right to make regulations for edification. And as the close friends of several among the Elizabethan bishops who had taken sanctuary at Zurich during the Marian exile, they proved an invaluable support to the bishops in their defence of the settlement against the extremists among the Calvinists. Against Geneva they appealed to Zurich : and as the Calvinists' pretensions to create godly discipline grew in the Rhineland, the Zurich fear of spiritual consistories and excommunications grew with it, and hence the open support of Bullinger and Gualter for the Elizabethan bishops. By August 1573 Gualter was almost an 'Anglican' in his way of talking. Before Bullinger's death in 1575 reckless men were unjustly charging him with receiving bribes from the English bishops. He did not die before he had explicitly condemned the proposition that the civil magistrate had no authority in ecclesiastical affairs. This support from Zurich was a powerful weapon to those seeking to defend themselves against Calvinist critics. Told that they must conform to the pattern of the best reformed Churches, the bishops were able to show that the very oracle of the Swiss Reformation did not agree with their critics.

In consequence the reputation of Bullinger with the English hierarchy rose to heights probably never attained since by any continental Reformed theologian. 'Yours, my father,' wrote Beza to Bullinger in September 1566, 'is the only Church by whose authority the queen and the bishops seem likely to be influenced.' And when in 1570 the pope at last excommunicated the Queen of England, she turned to Bullinger to publish the official riposte.

Bullinger's death in 1575 was not quite the end of the Zurich influence upon English bishops. For one of his pupils had become a leading theologian at Heidelberg, a man by the name of Thomas Lüber, better known to us in its Latinized form of Erastus: and at Heidelberg, confronted by a near-successful attempt to Calvinize the Palatinate, Erastus made the first serious effort, on grounds of scripture and reason, to prove that the Calvinist discipline, and the claim to intervene in civil affairs, were unwarranted. His theses of 1569, which circulated in manuscript, were first printed (significantly enough) in London in the year 1589.

Erastus, in Neville Figgis's phrase, was not an Erastian. But it was another proof from the school of Zurich that in following the pattern of the best reformed Churches, the Church of England might be aware of more breadth and more diversity in that pattern than some Puritans were claiming.

You will have observed that the main external impetus upon English thought came from Switzerland. And what, it is reasonable to ask, of Luther and the Lutherans? The relationship between England and Wittenberg which is apparent at isolated moments during the first half of the sixteenth century never became more than the decorous exchange of messages or theological conferences. It is true that the words 'mercy seat' and 'shewbread' are familiar words in the English language because Luther had translated the Hebrew equivalent by *Gnadenstuhl* and *Schaubrot*. William Tyndale when he came to make the first sixteenth century translation of the Old Testament adopted Luther's words into his own and so they have passed into the Authorized Version. It is true that some English works like Tyndale's *Parable of the Wicked Mammon* are derived from, and partly copied from, works by Luther. During the period when Henry VIII was feeling his political isolation, and when Thomas Cromwell was in power as his chief minister, Lutheran and English theologians met together to produce what are called the Thirteen Articles of 1538, some of which were to influence the later Thirty-Nine Articles. The English Litany owes something to the Lutheran litany of 1529. Archbishop Cranmer, when his cautious and scholarly mind was developing more rapidly under the new theological influences and the new liberty of the reign of Edward VI, took a Lutheran catechism, translated it into English, and published it without any hint to the public that its origin was Lutheran and with only three or four significant variations or alterations from the original. At the same time Cranmer was seeking to establish relations with the Lutherans and to persuade Melanchthon to come to England in order that he might hold an ecumenical conference of the leading Protestant churches, and thereby establish religious peace.

There are scholars who think that between 1546 and December 1548 Cranmer was passing through a phase where he had abandoned the doctrine of transubstantiation, but had not yet arrived at that Swiss doctrine of the Eucharist which he was certainly holding by the late autumn of 1548. The contention, if true, is very important because it is precisely those years in which Cranmer was drafting the first English Prayer Book of 1549, and therefore the argument over the Lutheran influence upon Cranmer affects the whole liturgical history of the Book of Common Prayer.

But we ought, I think, to be suspicious of this view that there is explicit theological influence upon England by Lutheran divines—at least after the very early period. No one doubts that Tyndale at one period in his life, and Robert Barnes from about 1526 until his execution, may reasonably be called English Lutherans. But in so far as 'Lutheranism' carries with it the doctrine of consubstantiation, or even the over-subtle discussions upon the ubiquity of our Lord's human nature, it is not possible to find Englishmen who were serious advocates of these theological proposals; and wherever English thought is not plainly in the Swiss tradition and not plainly in the tradition of the Counter Reformation, we ought to beware of therefore naming it 'Lutheran.'

The Puritans, during the reign of Queen Elizabeth, tended to label any one who held the doctrine of the Real Presence as a 'Lutheran,' and at the end of the reign they were even labelling as 'Lutheran' people who believed that it was possible to fall from justifying grace. But this was a mere label, and bore no relation to any actual influence of Wittenberg upon the people concerned. At the end of the century we find Samuel Ward of Cambridge grumbling into his private papers that Lutheranism was beginning to be maintained in the university. He did not mean that Lutheranism was beginning to be maintained. He meant that a Protestant divine, who was not precisely a Calvinist, had recently been elected professor of divinity. Or again, Bishop Cheyney of Gloucester and Bristol, who taught something very like the doctrine of a Real Presence, was accused of Lutheranism. There seems to be no suggestion that he had in effect been consciously imitating the theology of Wittenberg. He is to be compared rather with a humanist reformer (with a small rather than a capital r), like Cuthbert Tunstall, or even Stephen Gardiner at one phase in his life. These men believed in the reform of abuses and corruptions, and they wished to go a good deal less far in their effort at reform than the more radical adherents of Swiss thought. Men like Cheyney or Bernard Gilpin may readily be described as conservative reformers. What Cheyney declared to his congregation at Bristol Cathedral was nothing Lutheran. It was this : 'Be not too swift or hasty to credit these new writers, for they are not yet thoroughly tried and approved, as the Catholic Fathers are' ; or this : 'Follow ye the Catholic and universal consent. For if you will go to the river of the Rhine in Germany, and behold the cities, how they differ and are at contention among themselves, you will wonder.'

This moderate, reforming (but not Reforming) conservatism, represented by Cuthbert Tunstall to the right and Matthew Parker to the left, was not without its parallels upon the Continent. But the course of political events—the non-Roman Catholicism of the reign of Henry VIII, the papal reaction which in spite of the fires of Smithfield was somehow a tepid reaction under Queen Mary, the training of Queen Elizabeth and the need for politique and for national unity in her earlier years—this political history gave the moderate conservative-reformer an influence which he did not attain elsewhere in Europe. Moderation is a quality which allows tradition to be influential : and we ought to recognize the force exerted by tradition and the past even upon a Reformer who was not, at the end of his life, a conservative of this school, namely Archbishop Cranmer. It is true that Bucer and other divines influenced the history of the Book of Common Prayer. But that book was also affected by the *Antididagma,* a Cologne document designed to confute Bucer: by a Catholic liturgiologist like Cardinal Quignonez; and above all by the medieval rites. Bucer's work on ordination guided the construction of the Anglican Ordinal—and yet at the central point his guidance is deserted and the medieval Pontifical comes into its own. Though less marked, this is true of baptism, of confirmation, and of the liturgy itself. 'These new writers' of the Continent are seen to be of value, are utilized as eminent divines —but all the English did not lose sight of antiquity. The preface to the Ordinal includes a celebrated assertion : 'It is evident unto all men, diligently reading Holy Scripture and ancient authors, that from the Apostles' times, there have been these orders of ministers in Christ's Church—Bishops, Priests and Deacons.' It is a remarkable assertion. For if you consider the European theologians of the ministry in that year 1550, whether they were Roman Catholic theologians on the right or Protestant theologians on the left, you will see that this was *not* evident unto all men who were then diligently reading scripture and ancient authors. A concern for antiquity and for history has entered in, a concern shared by Cranmer and Ridley and Parker, the concern which led to the bequest by Parker of a magnificent historical collection to Corpus Christi College, Cambridge. During the last quarter of the century the revival of patristic studies in England—owing much, it must be said, to continental scholars like the Magdeburg Centuriators among the Lutherans or de la Bigne among the Roman Catholics—lent reinforcement to the moderate conservatives.

In the early years of Elizabeth, there was already talk of a mean, a moderate policy which should prevent the pendulum swinging too far, a 'golden mediocrity.' The critics of moderation preferred to call it 'mingle-mangle' : John Jewel thought it would have been better called 'leaden mediocrity' : Gualter of Zurich thought it was inventing 'a religion of a mixed, uncertain, and doubtful character,' 'an unhappy compound of popery and the Gospel.' It must be admitted that this compromise had little positive ground or content during the early years of Elizabeth, and we hear little enough about a via media. But with the political sharpening of controversy against Spain and Rome, and of the controversy against Puritan critics in the country, English divines began slowly to justify their moderation, and justify it by appealing to the ancient Church and to history. Here is the serene and unmistakable note of Richard Hooker, assured yet not aggressive—

'The Laws of the Church, whereby for so many ages together we have been guided in the exercise of Christian religion and the service of the true God, our rites, customs, and orders of ecclesiastical government, are called in question: we are accused as men that will not have Christ Jesus to rule over them, but have wilfully cast his statutes behind their backs. . . . Behold therefore we offer the laws whereby we live unto the general trial and judgment of the whole world. . . .'

The ancient and the modern, the tradition and the continental reform, have begun to dwell together. The bones of the medieval abbess, and the bones of the Reformer's godly wife, rest side by side.

5

THE SEVENTEENTH AND EIGHTEENTH CENTURIES

The Dean of Winchester

'THE BIBLE, I say, the Bible only, is the religion of Protestants.' The famous dictum of William Chillingworth was not written indeed until the seventeenth century had run more than one third of its course, but the principle which it embodied had been generally recognized and accepted by sixteenth-century reformers. *Sola Scriptura* however, instead of proving an unifying maxim, had been the parent of division; for their confidence that the Bible, once freed from the refractive medium of medieval scholasticism, would bear its one and only meaning so clearly on its face that he who ran might read, had been refuted by experience. Not only were Luther and Zwingli unable to agree on the doctrine of the Eucharist, but the career of Faustus Socinus had indicated the extreme of heresy in relation to the vital doctrine of the Trinity, to which reliance on Scripture alone might lead. Over against the schisms within Protestantism, the Roman Church had defined its doctrine and reformed its discipline at the Council of Trent, where, as the milk-white *Hind* of Dryden's satire remarked to the *Panther*

'The Council steer'd, it seems, a different course,
They tried the Scripture by Tradition's force,
But you Tradition by the Scripture try.'

Moreover under the impulse of the Counter-Reformation, Rome was not only stemming the triumphant tide of Protestant advance, but was recovering much of the lost ground. Why should not the Protestants likewise, taking a leaf out of their adversary's book, essay the experiment of a General Council of anti-Roman churches? Such had been the earnest desire of Calvin; such also

the dream of Cranmer; and such the opinion of Matthew
Parker; and the Church of England, situated *in via media*
betwixt Rome and Geneva, seemed particularly fitted for the
office of mediator and president of such a council. But, as the
Hind further taunted the *Panther,*

> 'In short, in doctrine or in discipline
> Not one reformed can with another join . . .
> Nor, should their members in a Synod meet
> Could any Church presume to mount the seat
> Above the rest, their discords to decide.
> None would obey, but each would be the guide,
> And face to face dissensions would increase,
> For only distance now preserves the peace.'

The justice of the charge could hardly be denied; for past
experience made it only too likely that a council of all the
Protestant churches would like a

> 'Polish Diet disagree,
> And end, as it began, in anarchy.'

Yet the imperative necessity of an united anti-Roman front, if
the Protestant cause were to maintain its position, was generally
agreed, and time moreover increased the urgency of the task.
The legacy of the age of Reformation to its successor indeed was
not peace, but division.

It was left to the seventeenth century therefore to make the
doubtful venture, and it was a further misfortune of Protestantism that the Synod of Dort was occasioned by another breach in
its defensive walls. For the fundamental bulwark of Calvinism,
the doctrine of double predestination, had come under challenge
in the person of the Dutch theologian, Jacob Harmanszoon, 'the
acute and distinct Arminius' as Milton called him, who, notwithstanding his education at the Genevan Academy and his work
as a pastor in that city, had later deviated from the strait path
of orthodoxy as professor of theology at Leyden University, and
by the time of his death in 1609 had formed a school of theologians to maintain his position. In 1610 his followers presented
to the Dutch Reformed Church a Remonstrance dealing with
five doctrinal issues, in which they rejected the doctrines of election and of reprobation, both in their supralapsarian and

infralapsarian forms; the corollary that Christ died for the elect only; the doctrine of irresistible grace, and the consequential belief that the elect could not fall from grace. In the following year another divine of this school, Conrad Vorstius, was appointed professor of theology at Leyden, and his nomination met with strong opposition from an unexpected foreign quarter.

In 1603 the crowns of England and Scotland had become united in the person of James VI of Scotland, who brought to his southern kingdom a strong predilection for episcopal polity combined with a staunch profession of Calvinist theology. In imagination he conceived himself as a kind of holy Protestant emperor, uniting the several Protestant churches under his own leadership and that of the Church of England. Moreover in 1611 he raised to the primacy an avowed Calvinist, George Abbot, in close sympathy with his own religious outlook. To James, the emergence of a new divisive force within Protestantism in the shape of Arminianism, constituted a grave threat to his dream of an united Protestant front. Accordingly, having read Vorstius' *Tractatus Theologicus de Deo,* he informed the States-General of his displeasure 'if such a monster receive advancement in the Church,' since 'never any heretic better deserved to be burnt.' Indeed James' only regret was that 'it was our hard hap not to hear of this Arminius before he was dead.' In these circumstances the king did all he could in reparation by having Vorstius' books burned at both universities and at S. Paul's churchyard, and by threatening to refuse permission to British students to go to Leyden if Vorstius' appointment were confirmed. When therefore the orthodox Dutch Calvinists replied to the Remonstrance by convoking the Synod of Dort in 1618 to determine the points at issue, James was delighted to co-operate in the work. Grotius indeed had advocated a Synod of all the Reformed Churches, but the States-General decided for a National Synod, to which however Great Britain, France and Hesse were to be invited to send representatives (a courtesy later extended to Geneva and Bremen also).

Four English delegates were therefore appointed, Bishop George Carleton of Llandaff, Dean Joseph Hall of Worcester, the Lady Margaret Professor of Divinity at Cambridge John

Davenant, and Dr. Samuel Ward, Master of Sidney Sussex
College, two of whose number, Hall and Ward, had been Fellows
of Sir Walter Mildmay's Puritan foundation of Emmanuel
College, Cambridge. James would have made short shrift moreover of modern critics who have alleged that these divines
represented not the Church of England but the king personally;
for he accepted the prestige and responsibility of his position as
Supreme Governor seriously. Amongst observers present at the
Synod was John Hales, chaplain to the English ambassador at
The Hague, who after hearing Episcopius' eloquent defence of
the Remonstrants, forthwith 'bade John Calvin "Good night".'
Not so the official English delegates, who accepted all the theological decrees of the Synod, whilst protesting against the intrusion of a statement affirming the parity of ministers which
they refused to subscribe. Notwithstanding, the doctrinal decrees
were signed, immediately after the president, his two assessors
and the two scribes, by the four English divines (amongst whom
Dr. Thomas Goad, precentor of S. Paul's Cathedral and one of
Abbot's chaplains, had replaced Hall who had retired owing to
ill-health), and by Walter Balcanqual representing the Church of
Scotland. Thus James had asserted the unity in matters of faith
of the Churches of his dominions with the Reformed Church of
the United Provinces, whilst championing both in Scotland and
England the episcopal polity and regimen. Nor was his controversial zeal confined to the rebuttal of Arminianism; for on
another front he embarked upon polemical exchanges with
Cardinal Bellarmine in defence of the position and orthodoxy of
the Church of England. Rarely could any Church have counted
upon so resolute a royal *Fidei Defensor*.

Of defenders of its faith indeed no Church had greater need.
Its position in 'the middle way' betwixt Rome and Geneva made
it the target of assault from both sides. Thanks also to James'
policy of attempted marriage alliance with Spain, and the actual
marriage of Charles I to Henrietta Maria of France, England
was exposed to a new and determined campaign of proselytism
from the Roman ecclesiastics of the queen's entourage. Individual
converts were made amongst the circles of the court, and two
Roman agents, Dom Leander a Sancto Martino and Gregorio

Panzani, were sent to England on missions of investigation and enquiry, from which there resulted on the one hand a series of reports which presented the Anglican position through rose-coloured spectacles and were unduly optimistic as to the prospects of corporate reunion, and on the other hand the tempting bait of a cardinal's hat to Laud. But Rome was interested only in the possibility of a return of England to the papal fold by means of concessions in matters of discipline; whereas Laud was conscious of theological differences which could not be composed until Rome became other than she was. Such controversial exchanges as those of Laud and Andrewes with Roman Catholic polemists can hardly claim to be regarded as establishing relations between the Church of England and the Roman Catholic Church, nor perhaps may the quasi-eirenical *Paraphrastica Expositio Articulorum Confessionis Anglicanae* by a convert from Anglicanism to Rome, Christopher Davenport, whose name in religion was Franciscus a Sancta Clara, nor yet the works in which William Chillingworth explained the grounds of his return to the Church of England after a transient conversion to Rome. These polemical exercises served indeed to delineate and defend the frontiers dividing the two Churches, though as yet the process seemed rather to sharpen than soften antagonisms, and the two sides scarcely came within distance of mutual understanding, not to say reconciliation.

At the same time the Church of England was brought into contact with the foreign Protestant churches in a variety of ways. Lancelot Andrewes conducted a courteous correspondence with the Huguenot, Pierre du Moulin, in which he maintained notably, and reinforced by his authority and learning, the position of Hooker towards these non-episcopal churches, recognizing them as churches possessing a valid, if irregular, ministry and sacraments, whilst urging them to restore episcopacy as the traditional polity of the Church since apostolic times. Theory was translated into practice in the case of individual presbyters of the foreign Reformed churches who were admitted to English benefices without being required to submit to episcopal ordination. In regard to cathedral dignities, being benefices *sine cura animarum,* the evidence is clear; as the preferments of Isaac

Casaubon to be Canon in the Eighth Prebend of Canterbury Cathedral from 1611–14, of Meric Casaubon to be Canon in the Ninth Prebend from 1628–71, and of John Gerard Vossius to be Canon in the Eleventh Prebend from 1629–44, sufficiently showed. With respect to benefices *cum cura animarum* the two classic instances of Peter de Laune, ordained by the presbytery of Leyden and instituted to the rectory of Redenhall, and Caesar Calandrinus, also ordained abroad by presbyters and instituted to the rectory of Stapleford Abbots, testified to the recognition of their ordination as sufficient. Nor should it be forgotten, as the illustrious examples of Hadrian Saravia and Isaac Casaubon made clear, that the *Ecclesia Anglicana* commended itself to foreign scholars, who had experienced the rigidity of both the post-Tridentine Roman Church and the Reformed Churches, as a true *via media*, characterized by comprehensiveness and a 'virtuous mediocrity,' as well as offering a haven to refugees from persecution. Such individual connections were doubly fortunate and fruitful.

But a new and unforeseen series of contacts with foreign churches was shortly to be the lot of many Anglican churchmen, when the overthrow of the Church of England and its episcopate and the proscribing of its Liturgy were effected by the Long Parliament. With the execution of Charles I and the establishment of the Commonwealth therefore, many leading divines went into voluntary exile. Those churchmen who accompanied the future Charles II to France found themselves subject to every kind of pressure, theological, political and economic, to apostatize to the Roman Church. For the prospect of a Stuart restoration seemed to depend either upon such a rebellion of the Scots as would, if successful, bring back Charles on terms dictated by the Presbyterians, or upon foreign armed intervention by the Roman Catholic powers of the Continent, and in either case the *Ecclesia Anglicana* would be doomed to extinction. Economically, the Anglican clerics had no means of subsistence, and sporadic threats were made to stop even their meagre allowances from the court as a way of accomplishing their conversion. Furthermore, theological argument was added to political calculation and economic sanctions. 'I do not remember in ecclesiastical history,' wrote one of their number, Richard Watson, 'to have read of any number of orthodox Christians chased out of their own country, at a loss for a safe communion in some one or other elsewhere; that [was] our special difficulty and misfortune.' On the other hand the Anglican exiles affronted the Huguenots by their unwillingness to make common cause with them. Never had the *via media* been so strait and narrow a path, nor so difficult to tread with safety and consistency. Nevertheless the cause of the Church of England was stoutly upheld by its exiled theologians. Cosin wrote his *Validity of the Ordination of Priests in the Church of England* and his *Regni Angliae Religio Catholica,* and Bramhall (well earning his sobriquet of 'Bishop Bramble'), his *Justification of the Church of England from the Unjust Aspersion of Criminal Schism* and his *Consecration of Protestant Bishops Vindicated.* There was no lack either of skill or courage in these defences of the *Ecclesia Anglicana,* at a time when in numbers it had become a veritable city of Zoar, 'a very little city,' and when its future seemed dark even to its most fervent disciples.

Other parts of Europe also received clerical exiles, who, wherever they went, upheld the traditions of their fallen Church. Dr. William Stamp at The Hague, extolling the English Liturgy, George Morley at Antwerp, reading divine service twice daily, celebrating the Eucharist monthly, catechizing weekly and performing the Occasional Offices as required, Bishop Bramhall in Brussels, preaching every Sunday, holding Confirmations and administering the Sacrament, two expelled Oxford dons, Richard Chalfont and Henry Tozer at Rotterdam, Thomas Marshall at Dort, Richard Maden and William Price at Amsterdam, Robert Creighton and Michael Honeywood at Utrecht, all were firmly resolved 'that they would do as they had done in England and they would have the face of an English Church'—though in a very different sense from that in which the Marian exiles had first used these words. Other divines went farther afield; a future primate, William Sancroft went on from Holland to Geneva, Venice, Padua and Rome; whilst Isaac Basire earned John Evelyn's eulogy as 'that great traveller, or rather French apostle, who had been planting the Church of England in divers parts of the Levant and Asia.' His travels indeed enabled him to cultivate friendly personal relations with Eastern Orthodox Churches, to leave behind memorials of the Church of England, and to sow the seeds of that mutual understanding which has matured in our own century. For at Zante he disseminated a Greek translation of the Catechism of the Book of Common Prayer, as likewise when he preached at the invitation of the Metropolitan of Achaia to his synod; at Aleppo he left an Arabic translation of the Catechism, and after visiting Mesopotamia he procured a Turkish translation for transmission there. In Jerusalem he established such friendly relations with the Greek Patriarch as to receive from him on parting 'his Bull of Patriarchal seal in a blank (which is their way of credence)'; whilst with the Latins he discoursed of the validity of Anglican Orders, and received from the pope's vicar there 'his diploma in parchment under his own hand and public seal, in it styling him *Sacerdotem Ecclesiae Anglicanae* and *S. Theologiae Doctorem.*' At Constantinople he even wished to have instructions from Prince Charles, authorizing him to discuss with the Patriarch 'proposal of communion with the Greek Church.' Finally, to round off his adventures, he settled for a few years at the invitation of the Prince of Transylvania as Professor of Theology in the Protestant faculty of the University of Alba Julia (Weissembourg). In addition Basire resided for a time at Smyrna whither, as at Aleppo, Anglicanism had followed the English traders in the service of the Levant Company. The care taken by the Court of the Company in choosing its chaplains at Constantinople, Aleppo and Smyrna is testified by their custom to require candidates to preach a trial sermon before them, as well as to produce certificates of good life and convinced allegiance to the Church of England. The success of their efforts is attested by the names of some of their chaplains (collected with details of their careers in Dr. J. B. Pearson's invaluable *Biographical Sketch of the Chaplains of the Levant Company 1611–1706*), such as Thomas Smith and John Covel at Constantinople, Edward Pocock, Robert Frampton, Robert Huntington and Henry Maundrell at Aleppo, and Edward Smyth at Smyrna; whilst indirect evidence of the calibre of successful aspirants is provided by the fact that the unsuccessful included William Lloyd, afterwards Bishop of Llandaff, Peter-borough and Norwich, and Sancroft's successor in the presidency of the Non-Juror episcopate.

When in 1660 therefore the Lord turned again the captivity of Sion, the clerical exiles returned in very different temper and churchmanship from those of their Marian predecessors who during their sojourn abroad had succumbed to the mirage of 'the best Reformed churches.' Furthermore the character of the Restoration church settlement reflected a marked sharpening and stiffening of the standards of churchmanship. The 1662 Act of Uniformity required episcopal ordination as an indispensable condition for the holding of any preferment in the Church of England, whether without or with cure of souls, and for the administration of the Sacrament of the Lord's Supper. These requirements closed the loopholes by which before the civil war members of the foreign Reformed churches had been instituted to English benefices without episcopal ordination. But the insist-ence on episcopal ordination provoked considerable misunder-standing and difficulty amongst continental Protestants, who, reckoning soundness of doctrine of greater importance than regular ordination, were affronted by the requirement of re-ordination of their presbyters by a bishop if they wished to officiate in the English Church, whereas Roman Catholic priests were not required to submit even to conditional reordination.

Notwithstanding, the latter half of the seventeenth-century may justly claim to have been one of the most ecumenically-minded epochs of Church history. Both in Europe as the effects of the Thirty Years' war were increasingly felt, and in England after the convulsion of the civil war and commonwealth, a more excellent way was sought for determining ecclesiastical disputes and differences. Contemporaneously there arose a strong reaction against the overdefinition of articles of faith which had resulted from the development of a Protestant scholasticism, characterized by the same elaboration of minor points of doubtful interpreta-tion as that of the authors of the Roman Catholic systems. Con-troversy between Protestant and Papist, as between the various Protestant churches, was concentrated now on the essentials of Christian belief and practice; and the court of appeal in both

spheres was widened to include the testimony of the early Church
in addition to the written word of the Bible. Thus there emerged
the concept of certain 'fundamentals,' common to orthodox
Christians of both Roman and Protestant churches, from which
attempts to extend the area of agreement might properly begin,
and which in themselves held out new hopes of success. Moreover
two of the most famous figures of seventeenth-century Europe,
Leibniz in Germany and Bossuet in France, lent the force of
their learning, authority and influence to the movement for
unity. Leibniz's *Systema Theologicum* in 1684 made such wide
concessions to Roman opinion on the doctrine of the Real
Presence, the sacrificial character of the Eucharist and the papal
primacy, as to earn the description of 'the closest approach that
Protestantism has ever made to Rome.' On the other side
Bossuet's *Exposition de la Doctrine de l'Église Catholique* in 1671
seemed to William Wake 'one of the fairest advances towards an
union that ever the Church of Rome yet offered'; whilst Edward
Gibbon, whose transient conversion to Roman Catholicism three-
quarters of a century later was effected in part by this work,
wrote of it likewise that 'in the *Exposition,* a specious apology,
the orator assumes with consummate art, the tone of candour and
simplicity; and the ten-horned monster is transformed at his
magic touch, into the milk-white hind, who must be loved as
soon as she is seen.'

In this movement towards unity English divines played a
prominent part. The age was characterized by devotion to
patristic study, an exercise which overleaped the boundaries of
church and creed. The Benedictines of St. Maur were extending
the fame of their house and the limits of scholarship, adorned
by such names as Mabillon, Montfaucon and Tillemont; the
Oratorian Jean Morin was revolutionizing accepted theories concerning the form and matter of ordination by showing that the
imposition of hands with appropriate prayer were alone essential
to validity; whilst Jesuits such as Petavius and Sirmonde added
lustre to their order. During the first half of the century in England Francis Young published at Oxford in 1633 the First Epistle
of Clement (which had been virtually unknown to medieval
scholars); and Ussher published there in 1644 his edition of the

Epistles of Ignatius, which Lightfoot saluted as showing 'not only marvellous erudition, but also the highest critical genius.' Almost a generation later John Pearson brought the contribution of Cambridge to Anglican patristic scholarship by his *Vindiciae Epistolarum S. Ignatii* in 1672, described by Lightfoot as 'incomparably the most valuable contribution to the subject which had hitherto appeared, with the single exception of Ussher's work.' A decade later still, in 1682, John Fell published his edition of the works of Cyprian of Carthage, which for two centuries held its place as one of the foremost of Latin Patristic texts, and which defended the Textus Receptus against the Primacy text of Cyprian's *De Ecclesiae Unitaté*. Nor were these exercises of merely academic importance. Their influence was great in an age when the claims of episcopacy versus presbyterianism on the one hand, and of episcopacy versus papacy on the other hand, were vigorously canvassed. Moreover a common study of the Fathers and a consequential respect for their authority drew together Anglican and Gallican scholars, in a mutual reverence for the Primitive Church as the standard by which to judge contemporary controversies and on which to frame a pattern for the unity of Christendom. For the Gallican divines represented a *via media* within the Roman Catholic church, as did their Anglican counterparts amongst those whom George Bull called 'reformed Catholics.' Each side knew and valued the works of the other and an international tradition of learning was established. Furthermore, patristic studies influenced doctrinal issues no less than matters of church polity, and Bull's *Defensio Fidei Nicaenae,* published in 1685 was welcomed by Bossuet as a powerful apologia for the orthodox doctrine of the Trinity, whilst his *Judicium Ecclesiae Catholicae* in 1694 earned the formal thanks of the clergy of France assembled at St. Germain, conveyed by the hand of Bossuet himself. The promising prospect created by this co-operation in the study of, and appeal to, the *consensus quinquesaecularis* was set back by the quarter of a century's military conflict between Great Britain and France between 1688 and 1713; for a state of hostilities then as now gravely impeded the free intercourse of scholars. Moreover when political circumstances made possible a resumption of learned correspondence, a majority of the earlier generation had died.

In England however, William Wake, who as chaplain to the English ambassador in Paris from 1682–4 had been both a spectator and actor in the earlier episode, was raised to the primacy in 1716, and immediately made it one of his principal concerns to revive and extend the former correspondence. As a young divine he had replied to Bossuet's *Exposition de la doctrine Catholique* by an *Exposition of the Doctrine of the Church of England,* in which he had set forth an eirenic statement of Anglican faith and practice on the particular points which had engaged Bossuet's attention. Whilst expounding frankly the positive teaching of the Church of England concerning the Real Presence of Christ in the Eucharist and criticizing Roman doctrine and practice in relation to the Mass, invocation of saints, the use of relics and images, and purgatory, he presented a conciliatory standpoint on such vital issues as tradition, the authority of the Church and the position of the papacy. In regard to the authority of the Church, he declared his belief in the indefectibility of the Catholic Church : 'this universal church is so secured by the promises of Christ, that there shall always be retained so much truth in it, the want of which would argue that there could be no such church ; we do not fear that ever the Catholic Church should fall into this entire infidelity.' So also the authority of General Councils was respected by the Church of England : 'and whensoever such an one, which we much desire, shall be freely and lawfully assembled, to determine the differences of the Catholic Church, none shall be more ready both to assist in, and submit to, it.' Finally he was willing to allow a certain degree of authority to the pope. 'When other differences shall be agreed and the true bounds set to his pretences, we shall be content to yield him whatsoever "authority the ancient Councils of the Primitive Church have acknowledged, and the holy Fathers have always taught the faithful to give him".' Herein also Wake was at pains to make clear where his own Church differed from other Protestants. 'Let those who are enemies to episcopacy and who deny any respect due to the chair of S. Peter, answer for themselves. The Church of England has both retained the one and will be ready, according to what we

have before declared, whenever it shall be requisite, to acknowledge the other.'

In the later correspondence which he conducted with two
doctors of the Sorbonne, Ellies Du Pin and Piers Girardin, Wake
was dealing with divines who stood much to the left of Bossuet's
position, and were therefore much readier to make concessions to
the Anglican point of view. Bossuet had insisted that Protestants
must accept the decrees of the Council of Trent as an indispensable condition of reunion with Rome and also the papal head-
ship of the Church as limited by the Declaration of Gallican
Liberties of 1682. The former condition was entirely unaccept-
able, since Protestants had not been represented at Trent and a
considerable number of its definitions had been directed against
them; whilst Bossuet held that the papal primacy was of
Dominical institution whereas Protestants could not concede
more than an ecclesiastical. Furthermore, Bossuet's attitude was
governed by the fundamental thesis of his *Histoire des Variations des Églises Protestantes,* that innovation was the characteristic of heresy and therefore of Protestantism, and invariability
that of orthodoxy and therefore of Rome. Du Pin accordingly
had fallen under the severe censure of Bossuet for his acceptance
of the principle of development in relation to sundry practices
and even beliefs of Roman Catholics, such as the use of images
and relics, the authority of the papacy, and the evolution of
Eucharistic doctrine. Worse had befallen him in the differences
between the Sorbonne and Rome on the question of Jansenism,
as a result of which he had been deprived of his professorship of
philosophy at the Collège de France in 1703, thanks to Bossuet's
opposition, and exiled by *lettres de cachet.* When therefore after
the deaths of Bossuet and Louis XIV and the reversal of policy
effected by the Regent, Philip, duke of Orleans, the exiles were
recalled and restored, Du Pin was ready to enter into discussions
with Wake on a basis of mutual concession and understanding.

In the important correspondence exchanged with the English
Primate, at the instance of Du Pin, between February 1718 and
June 1720, the most weighty single contribution was his own
Commonitorium on the Anglican Articles of Religion, Book of
Common Prayer and Ordinal. Wake for his part was insistent

that the Church of England was entirely orthodox in faith, accepting the three Catholic creeds, which he held to be sufficient for mutual recognition and intercommunion in matters of belief, and from which 'you will see how much we on our part ascribe to ecclesiastical antiquity and how far removed we are from those to whom the innovations of the last two centuries count for more than the venerable authority of the preceding fifteen hundred years. Certainly I would make bold to claim that, whatever other churches adhere firmly to the Vincentian rule, the Church of England is pre-eminent amongst them; nor will ever repudiate anything which has been believed everywhere, always and by every one.' Similarly the *Ecclesia Anglicana* had preserved an unbroken episcopal succession and the threefold order of ministry of bishop, priest and deacon, so that its ministry possessed both the apostolic succession and the essentials of valid ordination. On this point the archbishop was particularly emphatic, pouring out upon his Gallican friends memoranda, letters and books in defence of the episcopal succession. Moreover his ideal was unity without uniformity. Agreement on the fundamentals of the faith, which he held to be already existing, could consist with difference on secondary matters; in particular, intercommunion did not depend upon identity of belief concerning the Real Presence of Christ in the Eucharist, concerning which Wake was prepared as a token of comprehension to advocate the omission of the Black Rubric from the English Order for the Holy Communion if his correspondents on their side would abandon insistence upon Transubstantiation as a condition of communion with the Anglicans. To Wake, full *communio in sacris* could be effected without agreement in the details of Liturgy, belief and matters of discipline. 'In the meantime so far are they right,' he observed of Du Pin and Girardin, 'to distinguish matters of doctrine from matters of order and discipline, in which last national churches may vary without breaking the unity of the catholic church. But then they should in points of doctrine too distinguish fundamentals in which all ought to agree, from others of lesser moment, in which error or difference may be tolerated. And I am much mistaken if they must not at last come to the creeds of the first four General Councils, if ever they mean to restore peace to the Church.' Union and uniformity were two different things. 'I make no doubt but that a plan might be framed to bring the Gallican Church to such a state that we might each hold a true catholic unity and communion with one another, and yet continue in many things to differ. . . . To frame a common confession of faith, or liturgy, or discipline for both churches is a project never to be accomplished. But to settle each so that the other shall declare it to be a sound part of the catholic church and communicate with one another as such, this may easily be done without much difficulty by them abroad, and I make no doubt but the best and wisest of our church would be ready to give all due encouragement to it.'

In return the Gallicans offered corresponding concessions to the Anglican standpoint. The Sorbonne approved six points of particular importance to the Church of England; first that *adiaphora* should be mutually tolerated; secondly, that therefore the use of images was a thing indifferent; thirdly, that invocation of saints was not a necessary part of Christian prayer; fourthly, that communion of the laity in both species was to be allowed; fifthly, that the episcopate received its power directly from God, though provision should be made for subordination within the episcopate; and finally, that elevation was not necessary to the celebration of the Eucharist. Du Pin's *Commonitorium* emphasized and extended these concessions. In regard to the respective spheres of Scripture and Tradition, he affirmed that tradition 'does not set forth new articles of faith, but confirms and illustrates those things which are contained in the sacred writings, and defends them with new securities against those who think otherwise; so that new things are not affirmed, but old things from time to time newly expressed'; the most important example being the use by the Council of Nicaea of the word *consubstantialis* as a barrier against Arius. In respect of the authority of General Councils, Du Pin, whilst allowing that some Councils had erred, such as those of Ariminum, Seleucia and the robber Synod of Ephesus, maintained that those whose decrees had received the assent of the universal Church must be held to be exempt from error. On such minor matters as purgatory, images, relics and invocation of saints, liberty was to be allowed to each church to follow its own traditions. On articles of greater importance, such as the sacraments, he desired the question whether the five sacraments recognized by the Roman Church in addition to baptism and the Eucharist, had been 'instituted immediately by Christ,' to be laid aside, it being 'sufficient that they should be recognized as sacraments' by ecclesiastical usage and authority; whilst in regard to the doctrine of the Eucharist he was willing to abandon the word 'transubstantiation' if the Church of England would accept instead 'transmutation.' 'As regards the word *transubstantiation,* it is not necessary to retain that, if there is agreement concerning the thing. I should there-fore wish this article to be thus expressed. "In the Sacrament of the Eucharist, the bread and wine are truly and really trans-muted into the body and blood of Christ, and are truly and really received by those who receive the consecrated bread and wine, although this oral reception is ineffective unless accompanied by faith and holiness in the recipient".' Similarly with regard to the Eucharistic sacrifice, he averred of Roman Catholics that 'we acknowledge as one and perfect the sacrifice of the cross, by which Christ fulfilled and abolished all sacrifices, nor do we call the oblation of the host an unbloody sacrifice in any other sense than because in it there is a memorial of this sacrifice, and the offering of it is continued by the several members of the Church who offer together with the priest.' Concerning Anglican ordina-tions he professed himself 'unwilling for the ordinations either of English bishops, priests or deacons to be pronounced invalid, though perhaps some may be so; but there is nothing to prevent the Gallican Church from approving them, just as the Council of Nicaea ratified the ordinations (be it said without offence) of the Meletians and Novatians. If therefore an union is achieved, all the bishops, priests, deacons and beneficed ministers of the English communion shall be continued in their orders, functions, ministries and benefices, either of right or by concession of the Church.' Finally, the thorny problem of the papacy was met by a denial that the pope had any 'immediate spiritual jurisdiction' in any diocese other than his own; and by defining his primacy as consisting of 'this right, to watch that the right faith is every-where kept and the canons observed, and as often as they are violated to act in accordance with canon law to repair the evil. This is the sole jurisdiction which we ascribe to the Roman pontiff.' Du Pin's conclusion therefore was that concerning discipline and liturgy, 'there seems nothing in the Church of England whether in relation to its hierarchy, or ordinations, administration of the sacraments and celebration of divine service, to be reproved.' Accordingly the desired union of the French and English Churches could be 'effected, or at least set forward, without consulting the Roman pontiff. When the union is made, he shall be informed of it and humbly requested to give his consent. If he consents, the affair will then be finished, but if he refuses, the union will nevertheless be valid; and if he resorts to threats, then an appeal will be made to a General Council.'

Such extensive concessions might well seem to justify Bossuet's opinion of Du Pin, as being overbold and in a hurry. Certainly they represented a *rapprochement* between the Gallican and Anglican traditions upon which a practical scheme might have been built. But political and ecclesiastical circumstances, particularly in France and also in England, were not favourable to the project. Politically the regency of Orleans was precariously situated and in far too weak a position to embark upon so bold a venture. Ecclesiastically the Appellants or Anti-Constitutionists who had been antagonized by the papal bull *Unigenitus,* were only a handful of prelates, supported by leading doctors of the Sorbonne, but constituting a small minority of the episcopate and clergy of France. Moreover, and most significantly, Cardinal de Noailles, archbishop of Paris, carefully avoided direct personal involvement in the interchange of correspondence. Whilst giving good words to Du Pin and Girardin, he would not commit to paper one sentence of approval for communication to Wake. On his side also the English archbishop was at pains to keep the details of his correspondence secret from his brethren of the bench, nor had he obtained the formal permission of the king to enter into any negotiation for an union of the two churches. Had the matter reached the stage of seeking such official authorization, the attitude of the Hanoverian sovereign and of both his German entourage and his British administration might have been lukewarm, if not hostile; whilst in the Church Wake would have had to look for support to the High Church party from which on political issues he was aloof. Nevertheless the correspondence was of real importance as evidence of an eirenic spirit on both sides, and of the extent to which agreement could be reached on matters of faith, order and discipline, granted an appeal to the history of the first five centuries of the Church as determinative of points on which the two churches differed.

Concurrently with this development, the attention of the Church of England was turned also towards the foreign Protestant churches. The strict requirements of the Act of Uniformity of 1662 did not foreclose the possibility of union with the continental Reformed churches. In fact its provisions were explained to them as being partly the result of *raison d'état*, and partly the enactment of a domestic rule of the English Church, which, whilst demanding episcopal ordination for the performance of all ministerial functions within its own communion, did not either in intention or in fact pass any judgment on the presbyteral ordinations and ministry of any other church. Contacts between the Church of England and foreign Protestants during the half century following the Restoration settlement indeed were considerably increased by episodes of religious persecution and of conditions of war in several countries of Europe. The revocation of the Edict of Nantes in 1685 brought increasing numbers of Huguenot refugees to England, both ministers and laity, to whom Archbishop Sancroft gave a cordial welcome and for whom he sought to furnish both temporal and spiritual provision. Other refugees followed from the Piedmontese valleys, where the Waldensians suffered severely from the kaleidoscopic changes of policy on the part of the Dukes of Savoy during the Wars of Devolution and of the Spanish Succession. In their case likewise students and pastors were encouraged to receive episcopal ordination, since on their return to their own country such ordination would facilitate relations between their churches and the Church of England. Thus Bishop Williams of Chichester admitted to the diaconate in 1705 two brothers: *Cyprianus Appia et Paulus Appia, Fratres Pedomontani, religionis gratia suis sedibus pulsi, Oxonii studiis incubuere per multos annos, redditumque ad suos jam meditantes ad rem Christianam promovendam . . . ad sacram diaconatus ordinem . . . admissi sunt.* During the primacy of Wake the names of these brothers reappear as signatories of a number of appeals for financial help towards the restoration of their ruined churches and schools.

The most important, as well as the most romantic, example of the refugees from foreign Protestant churches, who came to Oxford for theological study and carried back to their own church and country abiding memories of the welcome accorded them by the Church of England, was that of Daniel Ernst Jablonski. Brought to Oxford in 1680 by Adam Samuel Hartmann, as a result of the foundation, thanks to the influence of Sancroft and Compton, of royal bursaries for the education in England of students from his school at Lissa in Poland, Jablonski became a member of Christ Church, where he formed particular friendships with the famous Dr. Fell and with William Wake, and from the former imbibed a lasting devotion to the works of Cyprian of Carthage. Coming over with the strongest prejudice against the Church of England, which presbyterian settlers in Poland had taught him to fear as a fellow-traveller with the Church of Rome, Jablonski in the course of his residence in England shed so completely these suspicions as to become an ardent admirer of the polity, liturgy and discipline of the *Ecclesia Anglicana*. Being himself a member of the *Unitas Fratrum*, he rejoiced to discover another reformed Protestant church which had preserved scrupulously the episcopal succession, and which, the closer his acquaintance became, proved more and more to be a model and pattern for his dreams of an union of all non-Roman churches. In 1693 he was called to the office of Court-preacher at Berlin and in 1699 was consecrated as Bishop (or Superintendent) of the *Unitas Fratrum*. Thenceforth his lifelong ambition and ideal was to unite the Lutheran and Reformed churches of the dominions of the Prussian king on the basis of a restored episcopate and a German version of the Book of Common Prayer; to effect an union of both with the Church of England; and thereby to prepare the way for the unity of all Protestants in an episcopal polity and discipline.

Into the details of his several schemes it is not germane to the present survey to enter. But mention must be made of the correspondence between Jablonski and Archbishop Sharp of York between 1710 and 1713 concerning the double project of introducing a German translation of the Anglican Liturgy into the royal chapel and into the cathedral at Berlin and thence throughout the Prussian territories, and of inducing the Prussian king to restore an episcopate in the apostolic succession through the agency of Jablonski himself and two English bishops. It was a proposal which appealed cordially to High churchmen, who welcomed the possibility of their church being directly instrumental in restoring episcopacy and a fixed Liturgy to the foreign Protestant churches. For a time also the Tory administration of Queen Anne seemed enthusiastic in support of the churchmen, but their zeal soon cooled and the good will of Prussia was sacrificed to Bolingbroke's passion for peace with France in 1713. Not until Wake became Archbishop of Canterbury in 1716 were the omens propitious for a resumption of the negotiation. Wake recognized the *Unitas Fratrum* as an episcopal church possessing an unbroken apostolic succession, and shared to the full Jablonski's zeal for godly unity and concord. Once again, however, after tortuous and protracted correspondence, the hostility of ministers of state, both the Hanoverian counsellors of George I and those of Frederick William I of Prussia, interposed insuperable obstacles and difficulties. In the sphere, therefore, of the two Churches of England and of the Moravian Brethren, where, thanks to their common preservation of an episcopal polity, the hopes of union seemed most promising, the vision faded into the light of common day.

Ecumenism however was part of the *Zeitgeist,* and amongst the Swiss Reformed churches a remarkable triumvirate of divines, Jean Alphonse Turrettini of Geneva, Samuel Werenfels of Basle and Jean Frédéric Ostervald of Neuchâtel, devoted their learning and eloquence to the promotion of Christian unity. All these were elected corresponding members of the twin Anglican societies, the S.P.C.K. and the S.P.G. In their own country they were the recognized champions of a tradition variously described as 'liberal orthodoxy' or 'reasonable orthodoxy,' which welcomed Wake's principle of the difference in status between 'fundamentals' and non-essentials in the domain alike of Christian faith

and practice. They deplored the rigidity of the theological con-
fessions which divided Lutheran from Reformed, and sought to
set forward unity on the basis of agreement in the fundamentals
and agreement to differ in *adiaphora*. With each of the triumvirate therefore Wake entered into long and cordial correspondence, pressing upon them the need for the taking of episcopacy
into their ecclesiastical polity as a means of setting forward the
urgently-desired union among the Protestant churches. If the
controversies dividing Lutheran and Reformed could be resolved,
the way would be open for intercommunion and in turn that
would be a step on the way to union. Wake urged upon his Swiss
friends, and they responded sympathetically, the tradition of the
Church of England as a guide and model; for its Articles of
Religion could be, and were, subscribed by churchmen of
Calvinist and Arminian opinions. But once again the endeavours
of the school of liberal orthodoxy were frustrated by the
suspicions entertained by the rigidly orthodox, and Wake was
drawn by his friends into the embittered controversy concerning
the *Formula Consensus,* by means of which Berne tried to force
the professors and pastors of Lausanne into acceptance of a rigid
Calvinist interpretation of the official confession of the Swiss
Reformed churches. In face of this controversy and the heat
which it engendered, Wake's ambitious project, shared by the
Swiss triumvirate, could make no headway. Ostervald at Neuchâtel made the most practical advances, by his introduction in
1702 of a *Catechisme ou Instruction dans la religion Chréstienne*
and in 1713 of a *Liturgie de Neuchâtel,* both of which deviated
markedly from Calvinist standards in the direction of the Book
of Common Prayer. The several Swiss churches returned fair,
indeed flattering, words to Wake in praise of the Anglican polity
and episcopate, recognizing its lawful character, the services
which it had rendered to the Protestant cause at the Reformation
and since, and acknowledging its Orders, but they did not venture any steps towards the conversion of their own presbyterian
system into an episcopalian.

The solitary practical issue of so much ecumenical correspondence was the recognition by the parliament of Great Britain in
1749 of the *Unitas Fratrum* as 'an ancient Protestant Episcopal

Church,' an act warmly supported by Archbishops Potter and Herring, though viewed with suspicion by Bishops Gibson and Sherlock of London. But not even this statutory recognition resulted in the establishment of official relations between the Moravian Brethren and the Church of England. As Ritschl observed of Count Zinzendorf, the tireless champion of the *Unitas Fratrum* in England, he 'did not succeed in laying the Moravian Church in the lap of the Anglican'; and when Bishop Gibson was approached by the Brethren on the ground that the two communions were sister churches, he replied somewhat sourly that, like sisters after the flesh, they would get on best at a distance. Moreover, after the middle of the eighteenth century the *vis inertiae,* characteristic of the age, overcame all endeavours towards ecclesiastical unity. Not until the Civil Constitution of the Clergy of 1790 brought emigré French clergy to England, did the Church of England resume its ecumenical vocation, and in this case the sympathy was of a practical nature and did not extend to ecclesiastical co-operation. Nor had the contacts established by individual Anglican divines with the Orthodox Churches of the East any practical results. Occasional visits to England of Orthodox prelates, chiefly of a mendicant character, did not produce ecclesiastical union, whilst the experiment of sending theological students from the Middle East to study in Oxford was short-lived. The Non-jurors indeed sought a formal union with the Orthodox Churches, but they were rebuffed by the demand for complete submission and acceptance of Orthodox standards on the one hand, whilst Wake formally disavowed them as schismatics on the other hand. The ecumenical ventures of the seventeenth and eighteenth centuries therefore were chiefly important as setting forward the cultivation of a temper of mutual understanding and *rapprochement* between leading scholars; and if the seeds which they sowed may yet grow into a tree whose leaves shall be for the healing of the churches, they will see therein of the travail of their soul and be satisfied.

6

THE NINETEENTH AND TWENTIETH CENTURIES

Canon H. M. Waddams

O N the 24 December 1799, the new Constitution of France was officially proclaimed, inaugurating the rule of the Consulate by which Napoleon Bonaparte became First Consul and ruler of France. England was at that time full of refugees from the French Revolution who had fled for their lives, and whose experiences had spread alarm and despondency in English circles. The radical nature of the Revolution and the intense hostility evidenced to all established authority, whether of Church or State, had some of the psychological results on Englishmen which the Russian Revolution was to produce 128 years later.

The eyes of British people were, therefore, turned to the Continent where they discerned dangers to their own stability and, even more direct, military dangers from the ambitions of the great French general into whose hands all power was concentrated. Bonaparte's policy at home was one of reconciliation and more than 150,000 refugees were allowed to return to their native land. Among them were many priests who were now allowed to resume their activities on promising to obey the new Constitution.

English churchmen followed with interest the fortunes of the Christians in France, and, although there was much hostility to popery, this interest was not by any means confined to the fate of Protestants. The convention, concluded between the French Government and Pope Pius VII on 10 September 1801, received attention in English papers, though they were not sanguine about the future of religion in France. 'How the struggle may terminate we do not conjecture but we fear that true Religion will gain little by the present change.' (*Christian Observer*, 1802.)

The religious climate of opinion at the beginning of the nineteenth century was not much affected by questions of relations between organized churches as such. There was an abundance of Christian activity which brought contacts with foreign Christians, and in these co-operation was welcomed from whatever quarters it came. On the other hand the outlook of most English Christians of that time was such as to lead them to regard the unreformed churches of the Continent as brethren who had not had the good fortune of receiving the same advantages in religious education as themselves, and a consequent readiness to share with others that enlightened approach to the Christian religion with which Englishmen had been blessed.

This was not surprising. When others are suffering from wars and bloody revolutions it is natural for those who escape them to count their own blessings, and perhaps to congratulate themselves on the sterling character of their own society. But it is not to be supposed that Christians in England were merely content to bask in the sun of their own good fortune. There can have been few periods which show so much successful voluntary effort to spread the Gospel. In this work it was common for members of the Church of England and of the Free Churches to combine indiscriminately. Clergymen of the Church of England often played the leading part in projects which were jointly undertaken, but this was the natural outcome of the preponderance in numbers and opportunities which were theirs.

Probably the most important event for the encouragement of closer contacts between continental and English Christians during this period was the foundation of the British and Foreign Bible Society in 1804. Its object was, as it is to-day, the spreading of the Holy Scriptures throughout the world without note or comment. Early in its history it began to provide Bibles in French and Spanish for prisoners and refugees in England. But what was more important was the rapidity with which the Bible Society aim was taken up in different centres all over Europe. Its activities, of course, extended beyond Europe, but there is no doubt that the close planning and contacts with other European

Christians which came about from common work in printing and spreading the Bible was a powerful factor in drawing Christians of European countries closer together. A reference to the influence of the Russian Bible Society was made only last year (July 1956) by Bishop Michael of Smolensk in a paper read to an Anglo-Russian theological conference at Moscow.

The final defeat of the Napoleonic threat in 1815 and the long period of peace that followed coincided with an immense increase of wealth in England, deriving from a successful industrial revolution. At the same time means of travel were becoming increasingly modernized. These factors combined to encourage a great increase of travel from England to the Continent, a practice which continued to grow throughout the whole century. From being an arduous, sometimes dangerous and always expensive operation, a journey to the Continent became first safe and easy, and then fashionable. Spas began to spring up and blossom forth ; young men went more and more to the Continent for their education and pleasure, like A. C. Tait, afterwards Archbishop of Canterbury, who arrived at Bonn on 22 June 1839, for three months' study, mainly on the subject of German education ; young women began to go abroad to be 'finished,' while their elders who thought themselves to be in need of a cure betook themselves to some fashionable watering place.

Besides the Bible Society there were other religious enterprises in which English churchmen and continental Christians co-operated. For example in 1817—according to its report of the year—the Church Missionary Society 'offered assistance toward the formation of missionary institutions in the continental Protestant states. In conformity with this principle, the Society has undertaken to supply that defect of service in the earliest Protestant Mission in India, established by the Danes in Tranquebar, which the distresses of the mother-country have occasioned. The Committee have also granted pecuniary aid to the Missionary Institution of Basle, mentioned in the last report.' The same Society was also recruiting missionaries from some of the continental countries and in the same year took some men into its service from Berlin.

The Society for the Propagation of the Gospel also had close

links with the Protestant churches of the Continent. It acted as
trustees for a large sum of money for the 'University of
Debritzen,' which ever since the Reformation had 'supplied
almost all Hungary with Pastors and Masters of Schools.' It also
held money on behalf of the Protestants of the Vaudois churches
the interest of which was for 'the religious uses of the Protestant
inhabitants of the Valleys of Piedmont.' (*200 years of the S.P.G.,*
p. 735.)

New English congregations began to be formed on the Continent and may be exemplified from a report of January 1815
(*The Christian Observer,* p. 62): 'Nor is this the only instance
in which Geneva has shown a marked respect toward the British
nation. We learn from the same letter, that "very lately some of
our countrymen being there, and finding themselves destitute of
a place of public worship, according to the rites of the Church
of England, joined with a few of the inhabitants in requesting of
the Council the allotment of a building for that purpose. The
Council received the request with tokens of great satisfaction,
and instantly granted it in a manner, and with expressions
towards our Sovereign and nation, truly gratifying. . . . At
present, indeed the benefit to be derived from this circumstance
depends very much on the casual presence of such English
Divines as may be visiting Geneva in their travels. Hereafter,
perhaps, as the English Congregation increases, it may be thought
advisable to appoint a resident clergyman, and thus to give full
effect to the liberal and unprecedented grant of the Genevese
Council".' It may be observed that the generosity shown in this
instance by the Council of Geneva was in subsequent years to be
paralleled in many other towns in Europe. The Church of England's ministrations to its people on the Continent have benefited
much through the generosity of local authorities.

During the early years of the century there was a fair amount
of public interest in England about the conditions of other
churches. Accounts of religious movements in churches abroad
appeared from time to time in the English religious papers, such
as the pamphlet which was noticed in 1815 giving a description
of the Waldenses of Italy. In 1821 an account received from the
British chaplain at Constantinople described the melancholy

event of the public hanging by the Turkish authorities of the Œcumenical Patriarch for his alleged complicity in the movement for the independence of Greece from the Ottoman Empire.

The first two decades of the century saw too the rise of another voluntary agency, the Society for promoting Christianity among the Jews. The agents of this Society in visiting continental cities often found themselves ministering to resident English people as well as pursuing the special aims of their Society. In the year 1818 a Reverend Mr. Way is reported to have arrived at Amsterdam where he found 'an episcopal chapel.' 'In consequence of an earnest desire expressed by many respectable inhabitants of the city, to have the service continued in the chapel by the appointment of an English Episcopal minister of piety and talents, a meeting was held to deliberate on the most effectual measures for attaining this desirable object; and Mr. Way was requested to transmit to the Committee of this Society a proposal, putting in their hands the appointment of a clergyman, who, with the discharge of ministerial duty to the British Episcopalians resident in the city, should unite endeavours to promote Christian instruction among its Jewish inhabitants. As their funds for the maintenance of a Minister to the chapel are small, they proposed that a moiety of his stipend should be paid by this Society.' (*The Christian Observer,* 1818, p. 861.)

The increase of the number of congregations of the Church of England on the Continent of Europe and of clergymen ministering to them obviously required that some regular episcopal supervision should be exercised over them. But for long nothing was done. In law these groups of faithful were the responsibility of the Bishop of London, but there is no evidence to show that in the early days of the century any Bishop of London took much interest in them. The absence of a bishop was particularly trying because of the need for Confirmation to be administered, and as a result of this need in France and the difficulty of getting anything done in England, the residents applied to the Episcopal Church in Scotland. The consequence was that, after a number of cautious enquiries, the bishops of that Church consecrated Bishop Luscombe in 1825 for work on the Continent. His letters of collation contained an interesting and significant phrase in view of the later policy of the Church of England towards the churches of the Continent : 'But we do solemnly enjoin our Right Reverend Brother Bishop Luscombe not to disturb the peace of any Christian Society established as a National Church in whatever nation he may chance to sojourn.' (Bishop H. J. C. Knight, *The Diocese of Gibraltar,* p. 40.)

Bishop H. J. C. Knight comments (*op cit.*) : 'Bishop Luscombe built entirely at his own expense a chapel at Paris in the Rue d'Aguesseau, officiating both as bishop and also from 1828 as chaplain to the British Embassy. Some few chaplains accepted his licence ; some declined to sever the older tie binding them to the Bishop of London, while those who wished to avoid all interference or inquiry were more easily able to maintain their independence when they might be supposed to have a choice as to their diocesan.

'When Bishop Luscombe died at Lausanne on 24 August 1846, no successor was appointed.' At that date there were 68 English clergymen officiating in North and Central Europe and Portugal, 27 licensed by the Bishop of London, 13 by Bishop Luscombe and 28 by nobody.

In April 1840 Bishop Blomfield of London addressed a letter to Archbishop Howley of Canterbury urging the necessity for a large increase in the colonial episcopate, and one of these needs, pressed in a public meeting by Archdeacon Manning among others, was that for a bishop in the Mediterranean. Thus it came about that the bishopric of Gibraltar was set up in 1842 and Dr. George Tomlinson consecrated its first bishop. This was a landmark for Church relations, for within the area of his jurisdiction were most of the Eastern Orthodox Churches, and the policies and activities of succeeding Bishops of Gibraltar had a most important bearing on the progress of the Church of England's relations with those churches, as will be seen later.

But the formation of the bishopric of Gibraltar still left the sheep of North and Central Europe without a shepherd nearer than London. Nothing strenuous was done about these chaplaincies until 1863 when the Bishop of London presented a report of a committee dealing with the supervision of congregations in foreign parts of Christendom not in communion with the Church of England. It is interesting to note that at that time the chaplaincies were divided into three categories : First Class—Embassy and Legation chaplains wholly paid by the Government numbering 7 ; Second Class—chaplains of Consular chapels partly paid by Government numbering 16 ; Third Class—the rest numbering 68. The report paid a tribute to the work of the Colonial and Continental Church Society and to the Society for the Propagation of the Gospel, both of which had undertaken responsibilities in the construction and upkeep of churches on the Continent.

It continued : 'Proposals have often been made for the foundations of a new bishopric for the superintendence of the chaplaincies in the centre and north of Europe, as the Bishop of Gibraltar superintends those in the south ; and no objection has been urged against this scheme, except that such few Church committees as at present act without submitting themselves to the Bishop of London will be even less likely to place themselves under a bishop of inferior power, and that many advantages are found at present in the ready communication which is kept up between the authorities of the Foreign-office and London House. On the other hand, the present arrangement has obvious disadvantages, arising from the want of personal visitation, and from the difficulty of securing a regular system for ensuring the rite of Confirmation to the young people of those English families who are permanently resident on the Continent.'

An observer to-day might reasonably comment that the objections are rather feeble and that close connections with the Foreign Office might be maintained without the necessity of depriving the members of the Church of Confirmation in order to achieve it. Moreover the evident success of the Bishop of Gibraltar in meeting the needs of his area would seem a conclusive argument to a detached onlooker. It was only in 1886 that a Bishop— T. E. Wilkinson—was appointed to look after chaplains in North and Central Europe. He was called 'Coadjutor' to the Bishop of London. The work is now done by the Bishops of Fulham.

During the debate in the Upper House of the Convocation of Canterbury on the report of the Bishop of London's committee two bishops, those of Oxford and Salisbury, stressed the importance of these chaplaincies for the progress of Church unity. By this time (1863) the idea of Church unity, and the possibilities of active steps towards achieving it, had a place in the minds of many people.

Meanwhile the Oxford Movement had begun and was gradually beginning to interest itself in problems of relations with other churches on the Continent. In the earliest years the Tractarians were too immersed in domestic problems to engage in extensive reunion work. Nevertheless their outlook was bound to raise reunion questions in a practical form sooner or later. There was an awakening interest in the Christian East springing not only from ecclesiastical motives, but also from travellers and from political events in the Mediterranean. Moreover 'the Tractarian Theory of the Church, tended to promote intelligent enquiry into the nature of Christianity in the Orient; for the Catholic world was held to exist in three Branches, of which the Eastern was one. Again, it was desirable to seek friendly relations therewith, since that would have removed from the Church of England the reproach of isolation. Furthermore, it was natural that these two Churches should draw together, seeing that Rome excommunicated both alike, and that they in their turn agreed in rejecting the Papal claim of Supremacy.' So P. E. Shaw wrote in *The Early Tractarians and the Eastern Church* (p. 76).

In passing something must be said about the plan for a Jerusalem bishopric, for though Jerusalem is outside the subject of this paper, the plan was conceived as an ecclesiastical and political collaboration between England and Prussia. A special Act of Parliament was passed and the first bishop appointed in 1841. The project has often been misunderstood as one to establish an Anglo-Prussian bishopric. This was not the case, it was to be 'an English bishopric with German congregations attached to it.' The moving spirit was an energetic and pushing tutor to the Prussian Crown Prince named Dr. Bunsen, who talked every one in Church and State in both countries into agreeing with the scheme—no mean feat.

The plan caused great opposition in England though there was no unanimity on the part of the Tractarians in opposing it. If it was this scheme which indeed caused Newman finally to secede, it seems additional proof that his secession was not fundamentally based on rational grounds but on emotional attitudes. The bishopric continued in its original form until 1886 when it lapsed and was afterwards revived by Archbishop Benson in a regular Anglican form. Before leaving the subject of this bishopric, however, it is worth quoting from the 'Statement of Proceedings' issued by the Archbishop of Canterbury the following paragraph concerning it : 'The Bishop . . . will establish and maintain, as far as in him lies, relations of Christian charity with other Churches represented at Jerusalem, and in particular with the Orthodox Greek Church ; taking special care to convince them, that the Church of England does not wish to disturb, or divide, or interfere with them ; but that she is ready, in the spirit of Christian love, to render them such offices of friendship as they may be willing to receive' : an important statement of policy.

A feature of the middle of the nineteenth century was the connection which was established between certain members of the Church of England and members of the Orthodox Church of Russia. They were begun by that remarkable man William Palmer (to be distinguished from the eminent theologian of the same name), who though ordained deacon in 1836, never proceeded to the priesthood. He visited Russia in 1840, the first of many visits to that country. His ability and sincerity were undeniable, but so were his wrong-headedness and tactlessness. For years he struggled to gain admission to communion in the Russian Orthodox Church as a means of establishing his position as an Anglican. He carried on a lengthy correspondence with Khomiakov, which was later published by W. J. Birkbeck, and in the end he was rejected in 1851, and four years later joined the Church of Rome. The way he treated the wife of Prince Galitzin, who had become an Anglican, was most severe. But the lady, who had strong Evangelical persuasions, was just as determined as Palmer himself not to give way, and she eventually won. But Palmer's hounding of her can hardly be called less than persecution. As the instrument for bringing the Churches of England and Russia together a less suitable person than Palmer could scarcely be imagined. But nevertheless he did an important work which was later to bear fruit. His controversies, his energy and his persistence brought the question of the relationship between the two Churches into the open, made people think about it and examine their own convictions and the reasons for them. And such thought must precede any earnest and serious attempt to promote unity.

Attempts to create closer understanding between Anglican and Orthodox Churches were given additional stimulus by the activities of the American Episcopal Church in the middle of the nineteenth century. The details of these fall outside the subject of this paper, but their importance should be noted. It was these American efforts which caused the great Metropolitan Philaret of Moscow to write a letter in 1865 containing these words : 'How greatly to be desired is the union of the churches. But how difficult it is for a movement, started with that end in view, to wing its flight with the desire pure and simple of arriving at the truth—a desire altogether free from any bias or partiality towards preconceived opinions.' (Athelstan Riley, *Birkbeck and the Russian Church*, p. 275.)

The cause which Palmer had begun was taken up in the second half of the century by W. J. Birkbeck. He made himself intimately acquainted with the leaders of the Russian Orthodox Church and with their thought and outlook. He visited Russia many times and never spared himself any trouble which would contribute towards greater understanding. He accompanied Archbishop Maclagan of York to Russia in 1897 and the previous year had been concerned with the visit of Bishop Creighton. By his writings and speeches he constantly brought the subject of relations with the Russian Church before the attention of his fellow-churchmen at home. He died in 1916, a year before the Russian Revolution temporarily put an end to the interchanges which he had so worked to encourage.

Contacts with other Eastern Churches were meanwhile being cultivated, especially by the Bishops of Gibraltar who found themselves in frequent touch with the Œcumenical Patriarch of Constantinople and with the other Orthodox Churches of the Mediterranean northern littoral. The first bishop, George Tomlinson, two years before his consecration, had travelled to the Mediterranean on behalf of the Society for Promoting Christian Knowledge with greetings to the Patriarch of Constantinople from the Archbishop of Canterbury. This visit was thought afterwards to have been a useful step in encouraging closer relations, although there were already friendly connections through the Embassy chaplain there.

Bishop Knight refers to this period as follows (*The Diocese of Gibraltar*, p. 57): 'The interest of English churchmen of this time was centred beyond all question in the Western portion of the Diocese, and in particular in Constantinople. The Crimean War served to heighten attention already aroused. It will be remembered that one of the objects of the foundation of the See was the maintenance and increase of communication with the bishops of the ancient Churches of the East. In 1847 the Bishop of Gibraltar was described as "not only superintending our congregations along the Mediterranean," but as "being the authentic expositor of the creed of our Church to the long-neglected Churches of the East," and as "considering this not his least important function." Constantinople, as the seat of the Œcumenical Patriarch, was thus naturally a focus of interest.'

In his episcopate from 1863–8, the second Bishop of Gibraltar, Bishop Trower, continued to foster these good relations. Indeed he even repressed his own natural desires in the cause of understanding, as was strikingly evidenced when some reformed Armenians wished to put themselves under his jurisdiction. It seems that Bishop Trower was anxious to fall in with their desires; however, he prudently consulted first the Armenian Patriarch of Constantinople. 'But,' we are told, 'while appreciating greatly the Bishop's frankness and straightforwardness, the Patriarch objected in the strongest manner. He declared that no words could express the injury done to his flock by the Independent missionaries, who had treated them as idolaters and had sown seeds of strife in families; that if this congregation obtained their request, their example in seeking it would probably be followed by others; and that if the English Bishop received them he would inflict serious injury on that ancient Christian communion. Bishop Trower accordingly followed the Patriarch's wishes, though evidently with some reluctance.' (*Op. cit.*, p. 72.)

This incident has some importance in extending to other ancient churches the principle which had been adopted, but not

so far put to a severe test, of not intervening in the life of those
churches and refusing to do anything which might savour of
proselytism. The influence of this attitude in building up good
relations with the Eastern Churches can hardly be exaggerated.
It is interesting to see that it was reciprocated in practical form.
'A Mr. Stephen Hatherly had received Greek ordination at Constantinople in order to minister to a few Greeks at Wolverhamp-
ton, and desired to increase the numbers of his flock. But at the
command of the Patriarch the Grand Protosyncellos peremp-
torily ordered him (27 February 1873) to abstain "from even the
idea of proselytizing a few members of the Anglican Church".'
(Op. cit., p. 84.)

It was, however, Bishop Sandford who in his long episcopate,
1874–1903, did most to improve relations with the Eastern
Churches in the Gibraltar diocese. He was assiduous in his duties
of calling on their leaders, and his visits were no mere courtesy
calls. He discussed with them burning questions of the day both
ecclesiastical and political : he explained constantly the position
of the Church of England, its catholic character and its distinction from the Protestant Churches. During his rule he was in
touch with the Œcumenical Patriarch and the Armenian Patriarch of Constantinople, and with Orthodox archbishops in all
the countries of the Balkans, besides Syrians and Copts elsewhere.

The results, or some of them, could be seen in the increasing
frequency with which the Orthodox were ready to attend
Anglican services. 'When the venerable Church Missionary
Society missionary at Syra, the Rev. F. Hildner, died in 1883,
the Greek Archbishop not only lent his cathedral for the funeral,
but attended it himself, gave an address, and the blessing. In
1875, at the consecration of the English cemetery at Smyrna, the
Archbishop gave an address on unity.' (Op. cit., p. 156.) These
incidents may seem small, but they indicated the breaking down
of misunderstanding and ignorance. Bishop Sandford referred on
a number of occasions to Orthodox assistance to his own people
in baptizing and burying them, and in giving them communion
at the hour of death.

His policy is summed up by Bishop Knight in these words
(op. cit., p. 164) : 'From the opening to the end of his episcopate

he set his face against proselytism, direct or indirect, in all forms. To detach members of the Greek and Roman Churches from the churches of their baptism he held to be inconsistent with the principles of the Church of England ever since the Reformation; to be a mistaken policy; to be a direct hindrance to internal reform; to be an act of intrusion and schism; to be a violation and outrage of the courtesy increasingly accorded to the Church of England; the creation of fresh wounds in Christendom instead of healing the old.'

The Eastern Churches and the Latin Church were not the only churches represented in the area of the Bishop of Gibraltar. In the western parts of the diocese there were vigorous movements of reform attacking the Roman Church in Italy, Spain and Portugal. These movements attracted considerable attention in England and many English churchmen wished them to be supported. The same stream of active Christianity which at the beginning of the century supported the Bible Society's work and made provision for the issue of literature for foreign Christians in their own languages was strongly disposed to encourage any movement of reformation in opposition to the Church of Rome.

There were within the nineteenth century three particular landmarks which affected the attitude of English churchmen towards the Church of Rome and in consequence towards other Christians on the Continent. The first was the re-establishment of the Roman hierarchy in England in 1850. This caused immense resentment in Britain and even led the Government to adopt legislation which proved too hasty to be lasting or effective. There was common talk about the aggression of Rome and a disposition to oppose Rome elsewhere.

But an even more serious event was the Vatican Council of 1870 and the proclamation at it of the Dogma of the Infallibility of the Pope when speaking *ex cathedra* on matters of faith and morals. Such a doctrine was of course anathema to non-Roman Christians. Particular resentment was caused by the claim of the Roman Catholics that this Council was an Ecumenical Council, and official utterances by Orthodox and Anglican leaders denied this claim and refused it recognition. The Vatican Council was also the occasion for a greatly increased interest on the part of

English Christians in the Old Catholics to whom there were, as a result of the Council, a number of new accessions, some of them notable scholars like Döllinger.

The third event was the condemnation of Anglican Orders in 1896 by the Bull *Apostolicae Curae,* which evoked the famous *Responsio* of the Archbishops of Canterbury and York. The decision gave added impetus to the tendency to draw closer to the Orthodox and Old Catholics whose Orders are recognized by Rome as valid as a living disproof of the papal claims.

In the diocese of Gibraltar in Bishop Sandford's time the question of his attitude to reformed movements in Spain and Portugal had to be settled. In 1868 reformers had established a body called the 'Spanish and Portuguese Reformed Episcopal Church,' though it had no bishop. An English Society called the Spanish and Portuguese Church Missions was closely concerned with their support and encouragement. In 1878 the Church consisted of nine congregations with four ordained ministers, formerly priests of the Roman Catholic Church. Failing to obtain a positive answer to a request to Bishop Sandford to take them under his jurisdiction, these congregations addressed a petition to the archbishops and bishops of the Church of England in that year. By them it was referred to the Lambeth Conference of 1878, which handled the matter very circumspectly and inconclusively. Nothing was done in the following ten years, and in 1888 the next Lambeth Conference considered the matter again and resolved that only 'extreme necessity' would justify the intrusion into the jurisdiction of another Church. In Bishop Sandford's opinions these conditions were not met and he therefore declined to act. But the Irish bishops proceeded to entertain the request of the reformers and consecrated Bishop Cabrera in 1894 for the Spanish congregations. The Portuguese (Lusitanian) congregations were not so favoured. Ever since that time the provision of episcopal ministrations to these churches has rested in the hands of a committee of Irish bishops, and, although voluntary support has been supplied from England, the subsequent history of those churches falls mainly outside that of the English Church.

The activities of the American bishops mentioned earlier was the occasion and perhaps the cause of official action on the part of the Convocation of Canterbury *vis-à-vis* the Eastern Churches. As a result of information on the subject the Upper House of the Convocation of Canterbury in 1863 appointed a committee, entitled 'The Committee on Intercommunion with the Eastern Orthodox Churches,' whose terms of reference originally were 'to communicate with the committee appointed at a recent Synod of the Bishops and Clergy of the United States of America as to intercommunion with the Russo-Greek Church, and to communicate the result to Convocation at a future session.' Chancellor F. C. Massingberd was appointed its chairman and it was his energy and ability which kept the subject before Convocation in the first years. The committee reported every year until 1880.

In 1865 this committee reported the formation of a voluntary body called the Eastern Church Association, 'the principle objects of which are to inform the English public as to the state of the Eastern Churches, and to make known the doctrines and principles of the Anglican Church to the Christians of the East.'

From about this time voluntary societies especially devoted to the furtherance of Christian unity became more and more important in spreading interest and enlightenment in England, and in providing an outlet for those who felt they wanted to make some sort of personal contribution to the work. The Eastern Church Association itself was united in 1914 to the Anglican and Eastern Orthodox Churches Union (inaugurated in 1906) under the new name of the Anglican and Eastern Association. This name was modified later to the Anglican and Eastern Churches Association which is still active. Together with the Fellowship of S. Alban and S. Sergius, founded primarily to foster relations between Anglicans and Russian Orthodox exiles between the two World Wars, the Association carries the main burden of voluntary work at the present time in promoting greater understanding of the Eastern Churches.

Another society which was to play an important part in the field was the Anglo-Continental Society founded in 1853. Its objects were: '(1) To make the principles of the English Church better known in the different countries of Europe and throughout the world. (2) To help forward the internal reformation of

National Churches and other religious communities, by spreading information within them, rather than by proselytizing from them; and (3) to save men, whose religious convictions are already unsettled, from drifting into infidelity, by exhibiting to them a purified Christianity, which they may be able to embrace.' (*The Official Year Book of the Church of England,* 1884, p. 218.) It issued a large number of publications, about 200 by 1884, in eleven different continental languages, and supplemented the work of the Society for Promoting Christian Knowledge in publishing translations of the Book of Common Prayer.

This Society which continued up to and during the First World War had as its secretary for decades the Revd. F. Meyrick (later Canon). It collected and distributed money. It raised for the Old Catholics an Austrian Bishopric Endowment Fund and made grants to all kinds of Old Catholic projects and persons. It helped priests who had left the Roman Church and who were in distress, relations with whom were not always easy. In its later years (from 1904 it was called the Anglican and Foreign Church Society) Bishop John Wordsworth of Salisbury was its chairman, and this was one way in which the bishop pursued his work for reunion.

It is not possible to mention even all the most important of the personalities on whom this work depended. But Bishop John Wordsworth was an outstanding figure in all the work for Christian understanding and *rapprochement.* He is especially well known for his work on Sweden, and his book *The National Church of Sweden,* the Hale Lectures for 1910, provided information which was not otherwise accessible in English. The episcopal polity of the Church of Sweden and the close resemblance of that Church in some particulars to the Church of England naturally made it an object of interest to English churchmen. An interesting sidelight on earlier contacts with that Church is provided in the S.P.G. history *Two Hundred Years of the S.P.G. 1701–1900* (p. 738). It also throws light on earlier efforts to provide episcopal supervision for the congregations of North and Central Europe.

'Besides assisting to supply and support permanent and summer Chaplains, the Society, in consultation with the Bishop of London, began in 1863 to make provision for confirmations in North and Central Europe; and by an undesigned coincidence, it happened in 1866 that the services of English, Welsh, Scottish and American bishops were engaged in visible unity in this work. The arrangement continued until 1884 when (its efforts meanwhile, 1867–75, to establish a bishopric for the purpose at Heligoland having failed) the Society was relieved of the task by the placing of the British congregations in those parts under the regular supervision of a Coadjutor Bishop, commissioned by the Bishop of London. Before arranging for a bishop of the Anglican Communion to visit Sweden, communication was had with the Swedish bishops, as it appeared that a licence had been issued by the King of Sweden in 1827, at the request of the then Bishop of London, authorizing the Swedish Bishop Wingard to confirm some British residents.

'These courtesies were followed by a striking scene of intercommunion in 1866, when Bishop Whitehouse of Illinois consecrated the English Church at Stockholm, and the Archbishop of Upsala (who had previously united in the Holy Communion) now attended with three other bishops of the Swedish Church and several clergy of the same, and delivered an address, closing with prayers from the Swedish Liturgy and the Benediction.' It is an interesting point that a Swedish bishop confirmed British residents in spite of the fact that in the Swedish Church it is not bishops who confirm but priests. It was an exceptionally friendly gesture on the part of Bishop Wingard. One might also ask, in passing, whether anything has occurred since those days to make such a notable act of intercommunion less proper. For the tendency of recent years has been to formalize relations with such churches as the Church of Sweden on a lower level than the action described above.

The Lambeth Conferences took a great interest in the Church of Sweden and welcomed bishops from that Church: its references to the Church of Sweden began in 1888 and culminated in the 1920 Conference in specific resolutions recognizing the Swedish priesthood and welcoming Swedish communicants to communion in Anglican Churches. Strictly speaking these were not acts of the English Church and therefore lie outside the subject of this paper. Nevertheless English bishops and churchmen were closely concerned and played an important part in forwarding them. The English Church took no official action about the matter until in 1954 the Convocations passed resolutions welcoming Swedish communicants to communion in England.

But, before further examination is made of the twentieth century, relations with the Old Catholics must be considered. Interest in the Old Catholics among English churchpeople began in the first half of the nineteenth century. The most important publication on the subject was *The History of the So-called Jansenist Church of Holland* published in 1858 and written by the great Dr. J. M. Neale. (Neale was also responsible for many publications about the Orthodox Churches and also for the translation into English of many excellent hymns taken from the Eastern Liturgies.) This preliminary interest in the Old Catholic Church of Holland prepared the way for closer association later.

The Vatican Council of 1870 provoked a crisis within the Roman Church and occasioned a split from the Roman obedience of numbers of Christians in Germany, Switzerland and Holland who afterwards formed or joined Old Catholic Churches in those countries. The story of the tensions of those days is a complicated skein to unravel, but this statement is sufficiently accurate, in spite of its omissions, for the purpose of this paper. When the Convocation of Canterbury repudiated the Vatican Council on 16 June 1871, it also sent a message of sympathy to Archbishop Loos of Utrecht. In the following year Bishop Christopher Wordsworth attended the second Old Catholic Congress at Cologne. His influence carried considerable weight at the conference, and had its effect on the terms of the Declaration of Utrecht, which was later adopted as the religious charter of the Old Catholic movement. Anglicans henceforward took a prominent part in the series of Bonn Conferences which concerned themselves with reunion problems and included prominent Orthodox churchmen as well as Anglicans and Old Catholics.

It would be wearisome to trace in detail the various visits, conferences and other contacts which over decades brought the Church of England and the Old Catholics of the Continent closer together. In 1908 the Revd. George E. Barber founded the

Society of S. Willibrord with the aim of bringing about closer relations between the Churches. Relations continued to improve up to the First World War, though with some tensions now and again, especially over the consecration of Bishop Matthew at Utrecht, a consecration which was afterwards officially declared to have been secured by misrepresentation and therefore to be null and void. But this did not prevent the bishop from starting a long line of *Episcopi Vagantes* in England. The confusion he caused has not yet been dissipated.

So far in all this account there has been very little mention of the Archbishops of Canterbury. The reason is not that they were uninterested in connections between the English Church and the Continent, but because during the period up to the First World War the Archbishops did not for the most part take an active hand themselves in these relations. They followed them with attention and were constantly consulted by the bishops and other leading churchmen who were engaged in them. Although they did not much appear in the public eye in the matter, no one who knows the Church of England in the nineteenth century could doubt that their encouragement was an important element in the prosperous issue of the efforts which were made. The Archbishops showed themselves detached and cautious at first, but as they themselves increased their personal knowledge they more and more helped on others in this work.

A definite change, however, came over the scene during the reign at Lambeth of Archbishop Randall Davidson. This was perhaps partly due to his own character and interests. His wide outlook and interest readily considered every kind of international question which was brought to his attention. But even more important than his own point of view was the First World War which was a watershed in so many ways; after its conclusion Christian co-operation and the attitude of the Church of England took on a new aspect.

In Christendom at large the last forty years have been most notable for the spread of what has come to be called the Ecumenical Movement, though if terms are to be used in their proper meaning everything which has been so far discussed must be considered to be part of an ecumenical movement. The First

World War brought home to many Christians the tragedy of their divisions and their helplessness in the face of divisive political forces. Archbishop Söderblom, the famous Swedish Archbishop of Upsala, by his energy and enthusiasm helped to launch the Life and Work Movement for Christian practical co-operation which had its first great international conference in Stockholm in 1925 and its second in Oxford in 1937. During the same period the Movement for Faith and Order had similar conferences in Lausanne in 1927 and Edinburgh in 1937. These two movements were later united and now form the World Council of Churches, which so far has had two world Assemblies, the first in Amsterdam in 1948 and the second in the United States of America in 1954.

Our subject would not permit an examination of the significance of these movements in the life of Christendom. It is, however, interesting to observe that all these meetings until 1954 were held either in the British Isles or on the Continent. In the formative years of the movement it could be said without exaggeration that the links between the English Church and the Continent provided a most important part of the raw material with which the finished product was made, and that it was leading English churchmen who often played a decisive part in the increase of co-operation and solidarity between the Churches. Of these in particular must be mentioned Archbishop William Temple, Bishop Arthur Headlam, Canon J. A. Douglas and Bishop George Bell of Chichester, a present Honorary President of the World Council of Churches. (He died in 1958.)

As regards the relations of the English Church to individual Churches on the Continent these became more 'official' in their character, not without loss. A decisive moment was the issue by the Lambeth Conference of 1920 of its *Appeal to All Christian People*. This created new opportunities for approaches of one church to another, and was officially communicated to the heads of all the important Churches of Christendom. As a result Archbishop Davidson found himself in the position of necessarily taking action as a result of the appeal. Such actions were part of the action of the English Church, even when from one point of view he was inaugurating something on behalf of the whole Anglican Communion.

The *Appeal* led to new attempts at understanding with many Churches. One of the most interesting was the series of conversations between members of the English and Roman Churches, generally known as The Malines Conversations. Archbishop Davidson gave cautious approval to the talks though not without misgivings, and they continued until 1925. Letters passed between Archbishop Davidson and Cardinal Mercier up to the time of the latter's death in 1926. A final conference to draw up a report was held in 1926 under the Cardinal's successor.

The conversations aroused bitter resentment among the Roman Catholic authorities in England who were affected by a combination of wounded *amour propre* and genuine anxiety. They wrongly felt that they alone of Roman Catholics in the world really understood the Church of England or were qualified to control any talks with its members. Largely because of this, and because of the protests which were made at Rome, the results were less than were hoped.

The attitude of the English Roman Catholic authorities has made it virtually certain that it would not be possible or advisable to try to hold any other talks on similar lines, and there is no doubt that it was a mistake to have kept them in the dark. Nevertheless the Conversations have had results, which are not without importance, though they are to be sought more in the effect on atmosphere than in agreements on paper. The Malines Conversations revealed to many continental Roman Catholics what some of their co-religionists in Britain would have liked to conceal, namely, that the Church of England is not just another Protestant Church like those on the Continent, that it has a strong Catholic tradition, that it has theologians of learning and integrity who appreciate the Catholic Faith whether in its Anglican or Roman form, and that it is genuinely anxious to seek the road of closer understanding and co-operation.

At the end of the First World War the Orthodox Churches of the East found their positions quite changed by the defeat of the Ottoman Empire and by the Russian Revolution. The Œcumenical Patriarchate of Constantinople also issued an appeal for Christian unity and the holders of the see, in particular the Patriarch Meletios, were anxious to promote closer relations with the English Church. In 1922 an official decision of the Holy Synod of Constantinople was communicated to the Archbishop of Canterbury in which was accorded what is commonly termed 'the recognition of Anglican Orders,' a somewhat misleading way of putting the matter. By this decision Anglican Orders were recognized as on the same level as those of the Roman, Old Catholic and Armenian Churches from the Orthodox point of view. This decision has not yet received the approval of all the Orthodox Churches though some have followed the example of Constantinople.

During the period between the two World Wars important official discussions were held in the framework of the Lambeth Conference with Orthodox theologians in 1930 and 1931, and with the Rumanian Orthodox Church by the Church of England. In 1925 a great gathering of Orthodox leaders, including two Patriarchs, came to London and celebrated the 1600th anniversary of the Council of Nicaea at a service in Westminster Abbey. Since the Second World War a theological conference has been held (in 1956) with the Russian Orthodox Church. This is an important step for two reasons. It is the first conference of its kind to be held with the Russian Orthodox, and it has provided the chance to fill the gap between the World Wars when it was not practicable to hold talks with the Russians but when conversations with other Orthodox had continued. In this connection it is worth remarking, in keeping with the fact that the renewed contact with the Russian Orthodox Church is a continuation of an interest of more than a century, that it is the Church of England that has provided the spearhead in taking up Christian contacts with Russian Christian people in recent years. The visit of Archbishop Garbett of York to Russia in 1943 was the first official visit of any foreign Church to Russia since the Revolution, and the latest theological conference is a new departure of promise.

It should be noted that specially friendly relations were established with the Serb Orthodox in and after the First and Second World Wars through colleges for the training of Serb exiles for the priesthood, established in England on each occasion.

The Archbishop of Canterbury in his relations with the

Orthodox Churches and other Churches of the East was guided from 1921 to 1932 by an Eastern Churches Committee which he himself set up, the Revd. H. J. Fynes-Clinton, a pioneer in Anglican-Orthodox understanding, being its first secretary. In 1932 as a result of two requests to him from the Church Assembly the Archbishop set up the Church of England Council on Foreign Relations to provide him with advice about all the Churches of the Continent and the Near East, and to forward such policies in relations to those Churches as were approved by the Archbishop. The first general secretary of this Council was Canon J. A. Douglas, who served it until 1945, and made a great contribution to solidarity and understanding with the continental Churches through his immense knowledge of personalities and conditions in the countries concerned.

With the Old Catholics official negotiations were taken up following a visit of an Old Catholic Delegation to the Lambeth Conference of 1930. The Old Catholics had formally accepted Anglican ordinations in 1925 and this cleared the way for new steps. Official conferences resulted in agreement on three principles for the establishment of intercommunion between the two Churches. It would be idle to pretend that the size of the Old Catholic Churches or their contribution to Christendom is very great in quantity. But they stand for an important principle of Catholicism without papal pretensions. From the point of view of the Church of England and of the reunion of Christendom the agreement reached between the two Churches is important as it established the basis on which the Church of England would unite with Churches of another tradition. The Lambeth Conference in its four principles for Christian reunion adopted in 1920 (the Lambeth Quadrilateral) for the first time had the chance of putting them into practice in an actual agreement. For this reason it is worth quoting the three clauses here :

'(1) Each communion recognizes the catholicity and independence of the other and maintains its own.

'(2) Each communion agrees to admit members of the other communion to participate in the sacraments.

'(3) Intercommunion does not require from either communion the acceptance of all doctrinal opinion, sacramental devotion, or liturgical practice characteristic of the other, but implies that each believes the other to hold all the essentials of the Christian Faith.'

Ecclesiastically in the last century the Church of England has felt itself closer to the Scandinavian Churches than to other Protestant Churches in Europe. This has been reflected in agreements reached with the Church of Finland (1934), Latvia and Estonia (1938), and the discussions which have taken place with the Churches of Denmark, Norway and Iceland (1954). The Church of Sweden had already been specially dealt with by the Lambeth Conference of 1920. These relations have all been expressed in resolutions of the Convocations admitting the communicant members of these Churches to communion in churches in England, and in the case of Sweden and Finland English bishops have on a number of occasions taken part in episcopal consecrations in their Churches and vice versa.

Questions of Christian reunion have become far more complicated during the last twenty years, especially since the Second World War, partly from the increase of the numbers of Churches engaged in plans for reunion throughout the world, and partly because the number of organizations through which relations with other Churches are affected has been greatly increased. This is an inevitable result of easier transport, and the much greater readiness, which threatens to become a serious danger, with which people can be gathered together for committees and conferences. The proliferation of such conferences may so blunt the edge of the instruments available for the work of reunion as seriously to lessen their effectiveness.

There is also a danger in modern developments that the tendency to do things officially will lessen the unofficial activities. This would be a serious disadvantage, for in the long run it is understanding and Christian love among ordinary members of the Churches that alone can provide a satisfactory basis for Christian unity. Changing social conditions mean that more people are travelling between England and the Continent than ever before, many of them for the first time. Those who are members of the English Church should be encouraged to take every chance of getting to know their continental fellow-Christians, their customs and their traditions.

The need for close association between the English Church and the Continent is greater than it has ever been. The Church of England has played an important role in bringing different Christian traditions together : it has no less a task in the future. There are welcome signs that the psychological atmosphere among Christians favouring greater unity is spreading and deepening. It is also true that Christians outside Europe are playing a larger part in Christendom. Yet in spite of the changes in power and centres of interest, it remains true that Europe and the Near East remain the centre of historical Christianity in all its main forms, and for this reason the relations between the English Church and the Continent will always be of significance to the Christian world.

The Second World War brought numerous temporary exiles from the Continent to England and Christian contacts between them and the English Church were many. At the end of the war the Church of England took a main part in raising large sums of money to help to rehabilitate the Churches of the Continent which had suffered from the effects of hostilities. Large numbers of refugees, fleeing from Communist oppression, have been admitted and have made their homes in England. For the first time in history substantial groups of Orthodox Christians are living in the country. As the beginning of the nineteenth century saw English Christians helping exiles from the Continent, so in the middle of the twentieth century there is another refugee situation in which the English Church is engaged in helping to meet the needs of continental Christians who have found in England a temporary or permanent refuge.

Abbo of Fleury, 17
Abbot, George, archbishop, 75
Adam of Petit Pont, 28
Adelard of Blandinium, 17
Aelfgar, earl, 19
Aelfric, archbishop, 23
Aelfric of Eynsham, 14
Aelfsige, archbishop, 21
Aelfthryth, daughter of Alfred, 19
Agatho, pope, 10, 12
Agnellus of Pisa, 38
Ailred of Rievaulx, 30, 57
Albert of Pisa, 38
Albert the Great, 39
Alcuin, 13
Aldhelm, bishop, 11
Aldulf, archbishop, 17
Alexander II, pope, 23
Alexander V, pope, 50
Alexander of Hales, 39
Alfred, king, 13, 14, 15, 16, 19
Allen, 64
American episcopal church, 104
Andrewes, Lancelot, 77
Anglican and Eastern Association, 109
Anglo-Continental Society, 109
Anne, queen, 92
Anselm, S., 27
Appia, Cyprianus, 90
Appia, Paulus, 90
Aquinas, S. Thomas, 39
Athelstan, king, 16
Augustine, S., 9f.
Austin Hermits, 38

Bacon, Roger, 39
Balcanqual, Walter, 76
Baldwin, archbishop, 36
Baldwin of Saint Denis, 18, 19
Barber, the Revd. George E., 113
Barnes, Robert, 60, 69
Barrett, William, 61
Bartholomew, bishop of Exeter, 36
Basire, Isaac, 79f.
Becket Thomas, see Thomas
Bede, 10
Bell, George, bishop, 114
Benedict of Aniane, 17
Benedict X, pope, 24
Benson, archbishop of Canterbury, 103
Bernard, S., 30, 31
Bernardino de Busti, 55
Bernardino of Siena, 58
Beza, 61, 66
Birkbeck, W. J., 103, 104
Blandinium, 16, 17, 19
Blomfield, bishop, 100
Blony of Posen, Nicholas, 55
Bologna, university of, 39
Bonaventure, S., 39, 44, 58
Boniface, archbishop, 11, 12, 14
Boniface VIII, pope, 40
Bossuet, 82, 83, 84, 85
Brakespeare, Nicholas, 28
Bramhall, bishop, 79
Bremond, Henri, 52
Bridgettines, 53
Brigit, S., 54, 56

British and Foreign Bible Society, 96
Browne, Robert, 61
Bucer, Martin, 65, 66, 71
Bull, George, 83
Bullinger, 62, 66, 67
Burgheard, 19
Burgred, king, 19
Burley, Walter, 49, 51
Byrhtferth of Ramsey, 14

Cabrera, bishop, 108
Caedwalla, 13
Calvin, 61, 66
Calvinism, 63, 66, 67
Cambridge, university of, 49, 50, 64, 65
Canterbury, Christ Church, 49
Canterbury, S. Augustine's, 11
Carleton, George, bishop, 75
Carmelites, 38
Carthusians, 54
Cartwright, Thomas, 64
Casaubon, Isaac, 77, 78
Casaubon, Meric, 78
Catherine of Siena, S., 54
Cenwulf, king of Mercia, 13
Chalfont, Richard, 79
Charles I, king, 76, 78
Charles II, king, 78
Charles V, emperor, 64
Cheyney, bishop, 70
Chichele, archbishop, 45, 47, 48
Chillenden, Thomas, 49
Chillingworth, William, 73, 77
Christian Missionary Society, 97
Christian Observer, 96, 98
Cicely, the Lady, 56

Cistercians, 30, 38
Clement VI, pope, 49
Clement VII, pope, 45
Clovesho, synod of, 12
Cluny, 29, 38
Cnut, king, 20, 22
Coenwald, bishop, 16
Colet, John, 53
Comestor, Peter, 39
Constantinople, Œcumenical Patriarch of, 104, 105, 106, 115
Council of Basel, 46
Council of Constance, 46
Covel, John, 80
Coverdale, Miles, 60, 64, 67
Cranmer, Thomas, archbishop, 68f., 71, 74
Creighton, Robert, 12
Cuthbert, archbishop, 12
Cynesige, archbishop, 23

Dante, 51
Davenant, Christopher, 77
Davenant, John, 76
Davidson, Randall, archbishop, 113, 114, 115
Dorne, John, 60
Dorothea of Prussia, 56
Douglas, Canon J. A., 114, 117
Dryden, John, 73, 74
Du Pin, Ellies, 85, 86, 87f.
Dufay, Guillaume, 58
Dumbleton, John, 51
Duns Scotus, 39
Dunstable, John, 58
Dunstan, S., 14, 16, 17, 18
Dutch Reformed Church, 74

Ealdred, archbishop, 23
Easton, Adam, 50, 51, 54

Edgar, king, 16, 19, 20, 22
Edmund, king, 20
Edward the Confessor, 18, 20, 22, 28
Edward the Elder, 15, 16, 20, 21
Edward I, king, 40
Edward III, king, 44
Edward IV, king, 54
Edward VI, king, 62, 64, 65, 69
Egbert, bishop, 13, 20
Elizabeth I, queen, 62, 64, 66, 69, 70, 71, 72
Elizabeth of Hungary, 56
Erasmus, 53, 60
Erastus, see Lüber, Thomas
Ethelred, archbishop, 19
Ethelred, king, 20
Ethelwold, bishop, 16
Ethelwulf, king, 13
Evelyn, John, 79

Fastolf, Thomas, 43
Fécamp, monastery of Holy Trinity, 18
Fell, John, 83
Figgis, Neville, 68
Fisher, bishop of Rochester, 53
Fitz-Ralph, Richard, 50, 51
Flete, William, 54
Fleury, 16
Frampton, Robert, 80
Frankfurt, 64
Frederick, William I of Prussia, 92
Friars, 37, 38, 48, 49, 50, 51, 54, 60
Folcard of S. Bertin, 18
Formosus, archbishop, 21
Fulk, archbishop of Rheims, 14

Fynes-Clinton, Revd. H. J. 117

Garbett, archbishop, 116
Gardiner, Stephen, 70
Gascoigne, Thomas, 47, 48, 53, 58
Geneva, 66, 67
George I, king, 92
Gerald of Wales, 35
Gerard of Brogne, 16
Gerson, 47, 56
Gertrude, Saint, 56
Gibbon, Edward, 82
Gibson, bishop of London, 94
Giles of Rome, 51
Gilpin, Bernard, 70
Girardin, Piers, 85, 86f.
Giso, bishop of Wells, 23
Goad, Thomas, 67
Goscelin of S. Bertin, 18
Gregory the Great, 9, 10, 11, 12
Gregory VII, pope, 31
Grierson, Philip, 18
Grosseteste, archbishop, 39, 47
Grotius, 75
Grimbald of S. Bertin, 14, 16
Gualter of Zürich, 62, 66, 67, 71
Guillaume de Machaut, 58

Hadrian, abbot, 10
Hadrian I, pope, 13
Hall, Joseph, 75, 76
Hallum, bishop of Salisbury, 46
Harding, Stephen, 38
Harmanszoon, Jacob, 74
Harsnett, Samuel, 62
Hartmann, Adam Samuel, 91
Hatherley, Stephen, 106

Haymo of Faversham, 38
Headlam, bishop, 114
Henrietta Maria, 76
Henry I, king, 29
Henry II, king, 36
Henry V, king, 46, 54
Henry VIII, king, 62, 68, 70
Henry Beaufort, 45
Henry, bishop of Winchester, 36
Henry of Easting, 49
Henry of Hesse, 55
Herring, archbishop of Canterbury, 94
Heytesbury, William, 51
Hilary, bishop of Chichester, 28, 36
Hildner, F., 106
Hilles, Richard, 64
Hilton, 54, 56
Holcot, Richard, 52
Honeywood, Michael, 79
Hooker, Richard, 61, 62, 72, 77
Hooper, 64
Howley, archbishop of Canterbury, 100
Huntingdon, Robert, 80
Hus, 46, 51

Incarnation, dating from, 12
Ine, king, 13
Innocent III, pope, 35, 36

Jablonski, Daniel Ernst, 91, 92
Jacob, Professor E. F., 45
Jacobus de Voragine, 56
James VI, king, 75, 76
Jerusalem, bishopric of, 102
Jewel, John, 71
John VIII, pope, 19, 21

John Capistrano, Saint, 58
John of Jandun, 50, 51
John of Salisbury, 27, 52
John of Wales, 52, 53
John Pecham, see Pecham
John the old Saxon, 16
Johnson, Francis, 64
Jordan of Saxony, 38
Julian, Dame, 42
Julian of Norwich, 54, 58
Junius, 61

Kempe, Margery, 55f.
Ker, Neil, 15
Kilwardby, Robert, archbishop, 39
Knight, bishop, 100, 104, 106f.

Lambeth Conferences, 111, 114, 117, 118
Lanfranc, archbishop, 18, 24, 27, 33f.
Langton, Stephen, archbishop, 39
Laud, archbishop, 77
Laune, Peter de, 78
Leander a Sancto Martino, Dom, 76
Leibniz, 82
Leo III, pope, 13
Leo IV, pope, 14
Leo IX, pope, 22
Leofric, bishop, 22
Levison, Wilhelm, 9
Leyden, university of, 74, 75
Lloyd, William, 81
Loos, archbishop, 112
Louis XIV, king, 85
Lüber, Thomas, 68
Ludolph of Saxony, 55
Lupus, abbot of Ferrières, 13

Luscombe, bishop, 99, 100
Luther, 60, 68, 73
Lutherans, 66, 68, 69, 71

Mabillon, 82
Maclagan, archbishop, 104
Maden, Richard, 79
Manning, archdeacon, 100
Marinus, pope, 19
Marprelate tracts, 63
Marshall, Thomas, 79
Marsilius of Padua, 50, 51
Martin V, pope, 45, 46, 48
Martyr, Peter Vermigli, 61, 65
Mary, queen, 64, 70
Mary of Oignies, 56
Massingberd, F. C., 109
Matthew, bishop, 113
Maundrell, Henry, 80
Mechtild, Saint of Hakeborn,
  56
Mechtild, Saint of Magdeburg,
  56
Melancthon, 69
Meletis, patriarch, 115
Mercier, cardinal, 115
Meyrick, canon F., 110
Michael, bishop of Smolensk, 9
Milton, John, 74
Montfaucon, 82
Moravians, 92
More, Thomas, 53
Morin, Jean, 82
Moulin, Pierre du, 77

Napoleon Bonaparte, 95
Neale, J. M., 112
Nicholas I, pope, 21
Nicholas II, pope, 23, 24
Nicholas Brakespeare, see
  Brakespeare

Noailles, cardinal de, 89
Nyder, John, 55

Oda, archbishop, 14, 20
Odda, earl, 18
Odo of Cluny, 16
Offa, king, 18, 20
Old Catholics, 112, 117
Osgar, monk, 16
Ostervald, Jean Frédéric, 92,
  93
Oswald, bishop, 16
Oxford, university of, 39, 46,
  49, 50, 64, 65, 94
Oxford Movement, 102

Palmer, William, 103
Panzani, Gregorio, 77
Paris, 38, 39
Parker, Matthew, archbishop,
  70, 71
Pearson, J. B., 80, 83
Pecham, John, archbishop, 39,
  49
Pern, Andrew, 65
Persons, 64
Petavius, 82
Peter Comestor, see Comestor
Peter of Candia, see Alexander
  IV
Peter the Lombard, 39
Petrarch, 52
Philaret, metropolitan of Mos-
  cow, 104
Philip, duke of Orleans, 85
Pius VII, pope, 95
Plegmund, archbishop, 20, 21
Pocock, Edward, 80
Potter, archbishop of Canter-
  bury, 94
Premonstratensians, 30, 38

Price, William, 79
Pullen, Robert, 28

Quignonez, cardinal, 71

Regenbald, 15
Regularis Concordia, 17
Richard de Bury, 49, 52
Richard FitzRalph, see Fitz-Ralph
Ridley, Nicholas, bishop, 71
Riley, Athelstan, 104
Robert, archbishop, 18, 22, 24
Robert, bishop of Hereford, 28
Robert Kilwardby, see Kilwardby
Robert Pullen, see Pullen
Rolle, Richard, 54, 56, 58
Rouen, cathedral church, 18
Rouen, monastery of S. Ouen, 18
Russian Bible Society, 97
Russian Orthodox Church, 116

S. Denis, monastery of, 18
S. Remigius, monastery of, 19
Sancroft, William, archbishop, 79, 90
Sandford, bishop, 106, 108
Saravia, Hadrian, 78
Schism, papal, 46
Sellying, William, 49, 52
Sergius III, pope, 21, 22
Sharp, archbishop of York, 92
Shaw, P. E., 102
Sherlock, bishop of London, 94
Sigeric, archbishop, 22
Sirmonde, 82
Smith, Thomas, 80

Smyth, Edward, 80
Smyth, John, 64
Society for Promoting Christian Knowledge, 92, 104, 110
Society for Promoting Christianity among the Jews, 99
Society for the Propagation of the Gospel, 92, 97f., 110
Society of S. Willibrord, 113
Socinus, Faustus, 73
Sonderblom, archbishop, 114
Stamp, William, 79
Stenton, Sir Frank, 13, 32, 33
Stephen, king, 29
Stephen Harding, see Harding
Stephen Langton, see Langton
Stigand, archbishop, 24
Stock, Simon, 38
Strasbourg, 65
Swyneshead, Richard, 51
Symons, Dom Thomas, 16

Tait, archbishop of Canterbury, 97
Temple, William, archbishop of Canterbury, 114
Theodore of Tarsus, 10, 12
Thomas Becket, S., 27, 35, 36
Thomas Gallus of Vercelli, 54
Tillemont, 83
Tomlinson, George, bishop, 100, 104
Tozer, Henry, 79
Trau, archbishop of, 50
Trivet, Nicholas, 52
Trower, bishop, 105
Tunstall, Cuthbert, 70
Turrestini, Jean Alphonse, 92
Tyndale, William, 63, 64, 68, 69

Ulf, bishop, 23
Ullerston, Richard, 46, 59
Urban VI, pope, 45

Victor II, pope, 23
Vitalian, pope, 10
Vorstius, Conrad, 75
Vossius, John Gerard, 78

Wake, William, archbishop, 82, 84, 86f., 91, 92, 93
Waleys, Thomas, 52
Ward, Samuel, 70, 76
Warham, archbishop, 53
Watson, Richard, 79
Way, the Revd., 99
Werenfels, Samuel, 92
Whitby, synod of, 10
Whitehouse, bishop, 110
Wilfrid, archbishop, 10, 12, 13
Wilkinson, T. E., bishop, 101
William, George, 28, 29, 31
William of Occam, 50

Williams, bishop, 90
Willibrord, S., 11
Winchelsea, archbishop, 40
Winchester, New Minster, 16
Wingard, bishop, 110
Wittenberg, 65, 66, 68, 70
Wordsworth, John, bishop, 110
Wormald, Francis, 15
Wormat, abbot, 16
Wulfric, abbot, 18
Wulfstan, archbishop, 20
Wulfwig, bishop of Dorchester, 23, 24
Wyclif, John, 43, 46, 48, 50, 51
Wycliffites, 43, 51

Young, Francis, 82

Zacharias, pope, 12
Zinzendorf, count, 94
Zürich, 63, 64, 65, 66, 67
Zwingli, 61, 62, 73